ADVANCE PRAISE

"I adore *Settling Twice*. Deborah Joy Corey's work is a singular joy to ingest."

—Andre Dubus III

"Reading this glorious book is like reading a constellation of stars. Each element shines alone, but eventually a picture emerges—a profoundly moving story of a grieving daughter and the incandescent family who formed her . . . I felt this one in my bones."

—Monica Wood, author of
When We Were the Kennedys, Any Bitter Thing, and *Ernie's Ark*

"Deborah Joy Corey puts a whole universe on the head of a pin as she considers a woman's many roles—mother, lover, wife, daughter, and sibling —and explores the loaded themes of creativity, sexuality, and spirituality in the harsh and beautiful world of coastal Maine. God is in these pages, which is something different and very damn interesting, in my opinion."

—Lee Smith

"Corey's dance between contentment and an inner sense of "unsettlement" is almost unnerving, striking philosophical truths that ricochet off the page and deep into the reader, forcing them to weight their own journeys against the remembered and oft-misunderstood journeys of their parents. A tour de force."

—Lavanya Sankaran

"*Settling Twice* is like morning in Maine: lush, clear, suffused with grace of nature, uplifting and ardent and deep. Deborah Joy Corey captures with insight and wisdom the delicate and fierce bonds of family, history, memory, and place in her artful and soulful prose . . . "

—Jane Mendelsohn

"*Settling Twice* is a book of quiet reflection, of wistful regard, where revelations of a family offer us the whole life of a remarkable woman. It is a book to be grateful for."

—Patrick Lane

OTHER BOOKS BY
DEBORAH JOY COREY

Settling Twice

LESSONS FROM THEN AND NOW

DEBORAH JOY COREY

ISLANDPORT PRESS

ISLANDPORT PRESS

Islandport Press
P.O. Box 10
Yarmouth, ME 04096
www.islandportpress.com
books@islandportpress.com

Copyright © 2017 by Deborah Joy Corey

All Rights Reserved. Published in the United States by Islandport Press.
International copyright reserved in all countries. No part of this book may be
reproduced in any form without written permission from the publisher.

This book is memoir. It reflects the author's present recollections of experiences
over time. Some names and characteristics have been changed, some events
have been compressed, and some dialogue and scenes have been recreated.

ISBN: 978-1-944762-18-6
Library of Congress Control Number: 2017933493

Dean L. Lunt, publisher
Cover and book design by Teresa Lagrange

Printed in the U.S.A. by Versa Press

Portions of this work have been previously published in *Image,*
Ruminate, Third Coast, and *Writers on Maine.*

For my family

I want nothing new if I can have but a tithe of the old secured to me. I will spurn all wealth beside. Think of the consummate folly of attempting to go away from *here*. When the constant endeavor should be to get nearer and nearer *here*.

—Henry David Thoreau, Journal 1, November 1858

Preface

Settling Twice began in a place of grief. I had lost my father and my mother six years apart, and although I had been running from their absence, I knew the dark hole of it was catching up to me. There was nothing else to do, but to stop. I rented a place where I could be alone, and there my grief encompassed me like a black cloud that comes in over the sea. That cloud sent me back to my past, and to memories of my parents, and eventually to the lessons I had learned from them. They say that every time you recall a memory, it is changed. I believe this, for family events and happenings are recalled differently by each of my six siblings. Still, they have been a great resource for me in recalling these stories, and although certain details may vary, we all agree on the incredible influence that our parents' lives had on us. As my older sister instructed me not long ago, it is important that you tell it the way you remember it. And that is what I have done by collaging my siblings and relatives and friends and pets, my dreams and hymns and nightmares, and my experiences. Some details have been nudged to protect the innocent, some to protect the guilty. Some scenes have been adapted, because none of us could remember them, or because to discuss our shared memory would have been too heartbreaking. Yet the truth lives on these pages as surely as I am alive and writing these words. What extraordinary people our seemingly ordinary parents were. What examples of love and integrity. In a world that has thrown Jesus out with the baptismal water, we treasure their example, and their love. It is still here with us. This is what we have remembered. This is our true memoir.

Part One

one

Anne of Castine is being launched this morning. She is gracious on the boat trailer, with a sleek, upturned nose and low-slung wooden cabin, two generous square windows to stern, and two smaller square windows to bow. Even her waterless stance is elegant, yet solid in her sureness, her unassuming strength radiating from her belly like that of a middle-aged, but well-trained fighter.

On the trailer bed, *Anne* sits a dozen feet above the paved pier, which also serves as the town dock and public parking lot. The boatyard owner, Kenny Eaton, is standing near *Anne*, goading a man. "Go ahead, get up on her. Go up the side, you can get up there." Kenny takes the man's elbow, leading, jibing, and pushing him closer to *Anne*.

The man, whom I presume to be *Anne*'s new owner if only by his diffidence, shakes his head while hoisting up onto the trailer's wheel, and then he goes up and over *Anne*'s side, still shaking his head as if he's submitting to a schoolboy challenge. Maybe it is reminiscent of a similar scene when he was young and being pushed across the dance floor to ask a pretty girl to dance.

Once safely on deck, he disappears into the cabin below. I picture him giving the thumbs-up, maybe even doing a little jig to celebrate having ascended up *Anne*, although he will probably not remember it that way. He will no doubt remember it as cruising, a word used for both sea and land, and an activity that my father said could stop time and expand one's understanding of things around them. Dad was an expert cruiser, not of water, but of woods, spending years of his life estimating the lumber potential of his own land and the forests of other landholders. He pronounced the word as it is spelled rather than transposing the sound of the *s* to *z*. Cruising: To travel at a steady or efficient speed.

It was a vocation that kept his body strong, his mind mathematical, a vocation where he found freedom while trekking through poplar and maple, pine and fir, a square compass hanging around his neck like a backstage pass to a mythical forest.

———

The air coming off the buoyant tidal Bagaduce River is somehow virginal, fresh and silky against my face and neck and décolletage, air that not only sweeps the skin, but penetrates like a thousand tiny stars landing and turning liquid, creating the desire to breathe deeply that washy aroma that smells slushy with a dash of sea salt. Its weight is less than nothing and it makes my brain buoyant, too, cleansing it with the redemptive qualities of nature. Is that what Melville meant when he wrote *the lovely aromas in that enchanted air*? Is that what he felt? My poodle Max lies on the dark-planked sail loft floor, a miniature apricot posed like a tiny Shakespearean lion in a bleaching splash of sunlight. Clearly, the air is affecting him, too, calming him, satiating him. His head is raised as if in worship, brown eyes sparkling, pink tongue hanging, panting softly. He is a faithful dog, never far from my side, not really a shadow, but a tethered friend. Always close. I ask him if he is happy and he blinks. Like me, he loves the sun. All winter long, we move from sun patch to sun patch, desperately trying to calm our damp-induced shivering. Once I read in a camping journal that Maine winters can be powerfully cold—that the whole humidity thing buggers keeping warm.

By March, it is impossible to remember how harsh winters melt into satisfying summers. By March, I'll leave Max behind to take my daughters to the beaches of the Bahamas or Bermuda or California.

One particularly cold morning last winter, it registered 45 below zero with the windchill. Rushing from the airport parking lot to the terminal before the sun had risen, I turned to see my younger daughter trying her best to keep up, tears streaming down her face.

"What is it, sweetie?" I called.

"The wind, Mama. The wind is biting me."

"Run. Soon, we'll be some place warm."

Run.

To me, beaches are the great equalizer. All my life, I have searched them out for warmth and healing. After my father's death several years ago, I lay on a Bermuda beach and wept for days, the warmth coaxing tears the way sun coaxes water from the earth. There on the pink sand that gets its color from the waste of parrotfish, the realization of his death bore into me. Such was the power of his dying, as powerful and physical as the most hostile Maine winter. Who, without having experienced it, could ever imagine it? And who, without having known the death of a loved one, ever expects it to cut so deeply?

———

In the warm enchanted air, a few men have gathered around *Anne of Castine*. Of course there is Kenny Eaton, and Ted who drives the huge boat-hauling truck, tall and regal enough to have been nicknamed Sir Ted by Kenny's grown daughters. His presence in a car or half-ton would be overwhelming. Cartoonish.

Three other men loosely circle *Anne*, one I recognize as Brad Tenney, a realtor who has shown me a number of houses in town. Often, I wonder if he recognizes my restlessness, since I already have a suitable home on Court Street. Maybe my searching has something to do with a feeling that has followed me all my life, a feeling that no matter where I was, my true self existed somewhere else. Even as a child growing up in eastern Canada surrounded by those woods that my father knew so well, the poplar and maple, the pine and fir, I kept my eyes to the hills, drawn to what lay beyond. Surely that was where my real life was waiting to begin, or was maybe already taking place without me, and I was simply the cutout which remained.

Of course, a move a few streets away from Court Street would hardly be beyond the hills of Castine, but maybe the change would be enough to curb my restlessness while my two daughters are growing up, something new to temporarily inoculate me. No scratching or plucking them too soon from this village they so adore.

Brad Tenney is a golden Lab of a man, good-natured, and I suspect, loyal. He embodies the best of the village, soaked with as much history as any local and capable of imitating all of the present or long-gone inhabitants, making him popular with many. Still he has the ability to move through the elm-lined streets light-footed and often invisible—an expert cruiser—his faded navy baseball cap, worn oxford shirt, and bleached khakis as good as any chameleon's skin. When he passes on the opposite side of the street, I sometimes do a second take and even then, I may not be sure if it is really him. Another glance might reveal the sidewalk empty. *A ghost of chance, a ghost of possibility.* They say if you live on a remote coast long enough, you become acquainted with both.

This morning, Brad is taking the occasional picture of *Anne* while chatting with the two other men whom I don't recognize—and that on this small peninsula is a sign of summer—strangers. *Pen-* is the word root for "almost" when forming compound words like penumbra and penultimate; *insula* is Latin for island. *Peninsula* is almost an island, and probably no word describes Castine better.

This small village sits at the end of Route 166, a two-lane road that stretches fourteen miles southeast of Route 1. Just before the village, 166 narrows, dipping between an inlet on the Bagaduce River and a grassy marsh, a section dug narrower by the English during the Revolution in order to keep their soldiers from deserting. I often imagine those soldiers hollowed out by war, feeling their lives were somewhere else, waiting to begin, or maybe already taking place without them. The cutouts of these soldiers still hover over the fields and forts and shores of Castine, their bodies now made of fog and mist, their lonely cries still echoed by the swaying bell buoy.

It is said that we bring two selves to this world, and two sorrows. The two selves are easy to imagine with a soldier. Surely one self exists where he originated, and the other exists where he defends. His two sorrows are often impossible to guess, though, for one must always know the man well to know his sorrows, and even then they may remain a mystery. So far the easiest sorrows for me to recognize have been my father's. While he lay dying, they were as obvious as the green-blue of his eyes, as replete as the tears that would mourn him—one sorrow being that he was leaving his adored wife, and the other, that he was leaving us, his children. On his gravestone, we had engraved WONDERFUL YOUR LOVE FOR US, words as simple as they were grand, just as he was. Standing at his burial, we saw our reflection in the black marble stone. A flock of grown children with their mother, weeping. Beloved.

———

At times, the narrow part of Route 166—now aptly called the English Canal—floods, making the village temporarily an *insula*. For some, this is a dream come true. More than a few Castinians have expressed the wish for a drawbridge at the canal, a registrar of sorts, with a gatekeeper to keep a record of those who come and go.

Beyond the canal the road curves up a gentle hill through a tunnel of maples and poplars, rising into a turn where a high and broad avenue opens, allowing one to drive through the sheared green fields of the golf course. The first street off this avenue is Main: a long broad street anchored by stately elms that shade the colonial homes and storefronts, all the way down to the place of gatherings and dockings and launchings, all the way to the town pier. Here, the terns and seagulls and pigeons patrol, fat and loud preachers, consummate gatekeepers of the sea, careening, screaming, screeching, scolding, and registering all who come and go. If the bottom of the sea is chaos, as scientists have said, then surely the life at its perimeter could be as well. Perhaps these birds are only echoing tremors from below, like faithful canaries in a mine-shaft, trying to warn us of things to come.

I have not been around boatyards all my life, nor have I ever spent time in an old sail loft, as I am doing this summer, but during my years on this almost island, I have watched enough boat launchings to know the way men move when they are part of a launching. I say *men* not to exclude my gender, but because it is men who usually gather, and have since the Gulf of Maine became the highway of choice when settled in the early 1600s by the French and the English. Then Castine was a Times Square of fishing and shipping, a harbor cut so naturally deep that it could have become similar to Boston or New York City, but now this once busy coastal intersection languishes in a kind of gracious limbo, never too far from the past and certainly never too close to the future—a trait of many of its dwellers, as well—a trait that often reveals itself at launchings. Locals look, step back, wander, drift, all the while keeping watch, but they never get too close to the boat about to be launched nor do they move too far away. In fact, most will only touch her if she is in some sort of trouble, and even then, they will do this as hesitantly as the new owner ascended *Anne*. They will do it with some reservation, as if between them and the boat hangs a cloak that should not be touched unnecessarily.

Kenny Eaton waves men away if they become too anxious to help at a launching, especially if he is about to man the boat alone. It's as if they are insulting this seasoned boat wrangler by assuming he needs some assistance, or maybe Kenny knows all too well the proper approach, fearing something may be lost once others needlessly touch her, their oily fingerprints staining the gossamer forever. I wonder if what they stand to lose is not something of the launching, but something of themselves. Maybe the ritual of approach is similar to the moves practiced by any person moving closer to a thing in which vigilant admiration has created love, be that a boat or a person, a village or a whale, a sail loft or an island. Maybe what we all stand to lose by touching things unnecessarily is simply the chance to be close. Who has not stepped too close to an admired thing, only to have it quickly disappear?

Kenny doesn't say much if others offer to help. He simply moves ahead to get the job done, often never acknowledging their presence. The same way he and other locals might not acknowledge a stranger or a summer person arriving year after year, or even a declared new year-rounder, for that matter. No, the declared must earn their right to this village, which among other things seems to have something to do with toughing it out for several winters in a row. Even my short winter breaks to beaches keep me from the inner circle. *A real Main'ah stays.* Perhaps only then will I become acquainted with the ghosts. And only then will the locals nod at me with true recognition.

Once I was told by a man tilling my flower beds that some locals had taken bets on me the first winter I arrived. *Yes s'ar, they didn't think you'd last.*

I found the comment both flattering and insulting. Flattered, that I had been noticed, but insulted with the conclusion in the comment. It was as if I'd been lumped with a series of unsuccessful settlers. And what about the ones who hadn't made it? Had they left on their own accord as some of my Loyalist ancestors had, floating their houses on barges farther Down East to Canada, or had some been driven away? There is no shortage of stories of coastal expulsions, just as there is no shortage of people coming to rob and pillage the Maine coast. Perhaps even more threatening to a local now are those who come to change what they find, fancying themselves more sophisticated. No wonder we newcomers must earn our right to be here. No wonder locals don't always speak, even though they have assessed our presence, as easily as they have breathed in the lush morning air.

At launchings with eager newcomers and strangers milling about, you can almost see the ticker tape of language racing through Kenny Eaton's head— *city boy, cheapskate, asshole*—language that sometimes sprays from him like the black exhaust from his rotting launch boat, *Isabelle*, with the yellow zigzag of lightning painted on her sides. But during an early-morning launch, one before six a.m., these fiery words have been rolled away as snugly as a man's sorrows, as snugly as sea mist in tied sails, and Kenny appears unflappable. Later when the day is hotter and busier and Kenny is being crowded, things may change, but if the launch is early, which seems to be the case for the most beloved boats, a calm is rendered. Within this placidity, men are free to do their dance of respect and admiration as long as they understand that tried-and-true but never spoken rule of launchings: *Do Not Touch Her Unnecessarily.*

Beyond the deck, a cormorant is floating. When I first slid open the wide glass doors to the Bagaduce River twelve days ago, he was here, floating and keeping his back to me, but like the locals, I knew that he was fully aware of my presence, his head turning from side to side to catch me in his peripheral vision.

The double-crested cormorant (*Phalacrocorax auritus*) is black with a greenish-purple sheen rendered from the oils that keep his wings from drying, and he is long-necked with an orange throat. No more than a sea crow, I find him exotic, and have given him the name Jinx. Sometimes I spy him flying beneath the clear water, darting from place to place in search of sculpins and gunnels, a speed demon appearing to fly much faster beneath the sea than above. Early in the mornings, we are often the only two present. In a recurring dream, I cling to him and fly, the oil from his feathers greasing my palms.

On the deck, I lie facedown on the weathered boards. The sun feels warm and silken. Shading my eyes, I look down through the cracks. Glossy emerald seaweed floats in the high tide like embellished wings over the rocks and wraps around the sail loft's soggy pilings, which are rotting from the constant tides. The briny smell is both ancient and fresh, a primal past mixed with maiden hope. What smell do I like better than that of morning sea musk? Only the immaculate smell of my daughters' faces.

Shaded beneath the sail loft is a world with sounds of wet lapping, laughing, giggling, and sometimes crazed cursing as wild as any seasoned boat wrangler's. Despite the constant tides, a fairy house that my older daughter, Georgia, built between two pilings over a week ago still remains. No more than gathered moss and rocks and wood with blousy sea lettuce propped on thin twigs of driftwood to make a partial roof, it is easy to imagine the fairies frolicking about. Georgia says it is a home for sea nymphs, which are her favorite because they rescued Hephaestus, the son of Zeus and Hera. Famed for his artistry, Hephaestus crafted works of wonder, such as Achilles' shield, embossed with dramatic scenes of life and death, joy and grief, peace and war, scenes similar to Castine's rich history.

A circular grouping of pried-open blue mussel shells filled with dried sea grass represents the sea nymphs' beds. If one should disappear or become damaged, Georgia will race over to the town dock and retrieve another from where they cling to the docks, just below the waterline. For some reason, the shade of the sail loft has protected this work of art—every bit as interesting to me as Achilles' shield—but that is not always the case. Yesterday, I accidentally knocked a blue water goblet from the sill of an open window. It shattered and sprinkled on the wet rocks below, ringing like crystal. When I went down, there was nothing to be found, not even a shard of glass. The dank world had swallowed all the pieces.

Had the glass been consumed out of curiosity or resentment? Had I offended this damp world, or is it simply a soggy Venus flytrap? Would the glass be released someday? Might I find a piece of it while walking up along the shore, dull yet transformed? Over the years, I have found old bottles, broken jugs, pieces of pottery, and even a headless doll. Once I found a man's worn black belt tied around a woman's battered red flip-flop, creating such a vision of violence that I could not bring them home. Instead, I left them as I had found them, tangled with one another on the wet sand.

Jinx floats under the deck, but doesn't look up, always the nonchalant lover. I suppose he's waiting for the sardines I sometimes toss, but yesterday I gave what was left to a seagull that was sunning on the rooftop. Hesitating at first, thinking the seagull common, and although I hate to admit it now, unworthy of the sardines that I had reserved for the exotic one.

To me, sardines are as satisfying as any caviar. My father and I often shared a tin while my mother attended prayer meeting on Wednesday nights. She despised their smell and would not permit them to be opened in her kitchen.

Dad and I ate them straight from the can, savoring their salty sweetness as they crumbled like sea cakes in our mouths. If our calico cat Sailor lingered nearby, we'd feed him one, too. After, we'd bag the oily can in plastic and stuff it in the bottom of the garbage pail in the shed. Back in the kitchen, we soaped and rinsed our hands thoroughly, as if the smell were a sin that needed to be wiped away before Mom returned. Still, she always knew. No matter what we did, she smelled their oily ghosts, and the scent annoyed her until it dissipated, a smell similar to the one on my hands when I wake from dreams of clinging to Jinx.

Yesterday, after listening to the seagull's desperate nasal *caw*, I lined several sardines across the deck floor, and then stepped back inside to watch him descend upon them. Within seconds, other seagulls flapped about, their white wings so powerful that the papers on my desk fluttered. Long I gazed at the prodigy of plumage. Watching, it occurred to me that I hadn't been captivated by a bird in a very long time. The thought opened like a dark and ravaged stage. *Who has not sat before his own heart's curtain? It lifts and the scenery is falling apart.*

Watching Jinx's shiny black head and breathing in his ancientness with the sea musk, I wonder when I lost my ability to see this world of living creatures. When did I stop seeing? When did I stop looking? My mother said that when I was three I could identify and imitate all the songbirds in our yard. The white-throated sparrow was my favorite. It sang, *Oh, sweet Canada.* Second to the sparrow was the ruby-throated hummingbird. I loved it not for its buzzing, clicking sound, but because Mom had once revived one chilled by frost. As a child, I ran the hummingbird's resurrection over and over in my head. Now I barely recognized nor noticed one bird from another. What dark stage was I standing on? Henry Beston declared in *The Outermost House* that nature is a part of our humanity, and without some awareness and experience of that divine mystery, man ceases to be man. Had I ceased to be woman? And had a glorious black crow come to restore my senses?

———

For twelve days, I had tried to coax Jinx closer. At low tide I sometimes sat under the sail loft on a rock, camouflaged with wet bubbled seaweed and tossing sardines one by one, but he had retrieved them all without looking at me. Why was his presence not enough? Why did I need to be acknowledged?

Snorkeling in the Bahamas, I once came across a barracuda. It suddenly appeared within arm's reach, metal gray and floating sideways. About three feet long, he was shaped like a small shark with a frowning, disapproving mouth. My husband had warned me if I saw a barracuda to pop it on its nose with my diving stick, but I could not. How could I move when I could not breathe? The clear greenish eye held me spellbound as if within it lay a work of wonder and all I needed to witness it was to be present. The barracuda and I stayed eye to eye for what seemed like a very long time. When he turned to scoot away, the sea carried his whisper, *Know me.*

Back in the beach house, I pored over the section on barracudas in *Fish of the Atlantic*—a fierce fish with a narrow muscular body, a long cruel mouth with undershot jaw, and yellowish-green eyes. Barracudas will strike at most moving objects. Swimmers have been fatally bitten by them. How exhilarating to know that I'd come so close and not been bitten. I had my own survival story to tell. And I'd concluded that it was my stillness that had saved me—not a diving stick, but being held spellbound.

I told the barracuda story over and over. So often, that on another trip to the Bahamas, my husband visited a local goldsmith and had a small gold barracuda necklace made for me. That was long ago. When I think how few times I have been held spellbound by nature in the last twenty years, I feel ashamed. But in the memory of the barracuda, I find something else shameful. The telling and retelling of my story had diluted the experience somehow, worn it out from too much touching, like the feet of Saint Peter at the Vatican's door. Now, I only remember my story and not the intoxicating feeling of being present with the barracuda.

As if to reassure me, Max comes closer, his toenails clicking on the deck. He stands still, looking down through the cracks, too. Maybe he feels the innate possibility of Jinx's power over me, or maybe he just wants to be with me. Present. "Oh, Max, isn't Jinx lovely?"

And you are too, my love, my penultimate, you are lovely, too.

Kenny hollers for his partner Ted and they walk around the boat trailer that cradles *Anne*, checking lines while the seagulls careen.

"Brings back memories," one of the witnesses says, as if to no one and as if to all.

"Oh yeah."

"Nice one."

Even though I am only a short distance from these men, I cannot tell which sentence belongs to whom. No, these voices are communal in their intimacy with *Anne of Castine*, as communal and indistinguishable as voices singing while countless hands pull on a rope to raise a sail. *Hooray, and up she rises, Early in the morning . . .*

If this time transcends everyday life as some occasions do, these men may look at their palms later and see marks from their communal moment. A Salinger character said, "I have scars on my hands from touching certain people." If nature is part of our humanity, then maybe we are capable of being marked by it as well. And if this is possible, then maybe we can also be marked by the inanimate things that we love, by boats and sail lofts, by islands and villages.

When a dear friend reminded me of the Salinger line not long ago, I asked her what it meant. Not that I didn't understand, but for a moment the beauty of it was overwhelming, a statement immense enough to make me stop in its penumbra, as powerful and pretty as vast sails being raised above. Immediately I looked at my palms, studying the lines that some believe to be our past and future, but may simply be scars from touching certain people, or from having been present with the things that we adore.

I rub my palm lines, claiming the longest ones for my now-deceased mother and father. Always with me. With me still. I give three connected lines shaped like a perfect sail to my husband and our two daughters, and six deeply cut ones to my siblings and their children. Several I reserve for aunts and uncles and cousins and dear friends, and a few curving lines I name after my favorite beaches: Horse Shoe and White Sand and Big Sur. A circular line I give to my childhood swimming hole, one to a beloved pony, one for my first cat, the calico named Sailor, and one for a dog named Duchess, and then I claim a series of small X-shaped marks for all the songbirds that I once knew.

Perhaps some of the men gathered around *Anne of Castine* have been scarred by her. Maybe some have owned her or simply cruised aboard her once or twice, or maybe only watched her and collected photos as Brad Tenney is doing now, photos that will no doubt jog his memory in the years to come, memories of salty sea spray and sun and of crisp sails, and of words woven with his past.

Nice one, nice one, nice one.

The *Nice one* chant is encouraging enough to bring *Anne's* possibly still-dancing yet reticent owner up from her cabin and back on deck. No matter what he has left below, he comes to gather their praises, and no matter what he has felt in his lifetime, it is clear that he is beginning to relax aboard *Anne*, clear that he has breathed in her enticing musk. For the first time, I notice that he has a beard as wild and bushy as any seafaring captain's ever was. I hadn't noticed earlier, yet it seems so obvious now, so much a part of his sudden-easy stance. Maybe he is tired from dancing below, or perhaps it is the stance of having arrived or of standing on a long-awaited precipice. Maybe his past has been momentarily washed away or slightly altered, and is now pure in memory, making way for his future. A character in an Arthur Miller play remarked, *The past is holy.* Later, an essayist studying the play asked, *Why? Why is the past holy?*

Not merely because the present contains the past, but because a moral world depends on an acceptance of the notion of causality, on an acknowledgment that we are responsible for, and a product of, our actions.

In other words, there are no accidents. The scars we carry, if any, are not coincidental. We choose them, and then we leave this world, with or without them.

Are these scarred palms our redemption?

Were not the scarred palms of Jesus capable of redeeming the entire world?

Anne's owner grins as he listens to the others, gradually taking in something of his good fortune, being aboard her. It shows in his relaxed hips, his chin lifted, looking outward instead of downward. He is standing near the tiller, but not touching it, not unless the need be. Unlike earlier when he clung so climbing aboard *Anne*, he is clearly more comfortable now—the gossamer all but visible and swaying between them—vigilant familiarity becoming love. Maybe she is the accumulation of all his longings: his school-dance crushes, his longing to be comfortable, his search for redemptive, cleansing air. I don't know if he has scarred palms from touching certain people or from having been touched by nature, but if not, *Anne* may unclench his fists, just as the beseeching seagull on the rooftop unclenched mine. Maybe his redemption has never been closer or further away. I only see that now he is easy in his deck shoes and in this morning, and he appears to not be of it—in it, but not of it—cupped in the womb of *Anne's* apparent strength, encircled but not confined, her lines tossed loosely, and even though she is still fastened to the trailer, high and dry, it is clear that things are shifting before they even christen the shore.

It occurs to me that *Anne* is quite ordinary, almost simple in her design. That she, like the old sail loft that I plan to use as my writing studio this summer, is bare in the most beautiful way. Touched by so many, yet hardly changed. Worn, yet still strong, although her pilings are rotting. They say the sweetest of wines are immeasurably enriched by a mold that rots the grapes before they are pressed. The winemakers call the mold *noble rot*. And *noble* seems the perfect word for *Anne*, and for the sail loft, too. Even though they are ordinary, almost simple, they exhibit innately superior qualities. Qualities that are palpable.

Repeatedly, a deep breath taken and smelling of sodden timbers feels as if it is sending me into the past, and at the same time, guiding me toward the future. If the odds are ninety-nine percent that any given breath taken holds at least one molecule of air that was breathed by Caesar and Christ, then no doubt anything is possible. How could one help but contemplate redemption?

Jinx begins flapping and drying his wings, and then pulls out from under the deck. With his beak held high, he looks insulted at having to share my attention with the launching, or maybe he's annoyed that I haven't dropped any sardines. He flaps his plated wings that resemble armor and lifts off, rising over the Bagaduce toward the islands, his long neck showing a slight crook, his orange gullet gleaming. No one really knows a bird until they have seen it in flight, Beston declared. In Jinx's departing and then disappearing, he too seems to be saying *Know me*—the same words whispered by the barracuda's departure so long ago. I scoot back against the front of the sail loft and shade my eyes. He is and then he isn't. Just sky.

Anne's admirers are now communally quiet. They step back, giving her a wide berth. She and her captain are clearly partnered now. She, part of his future and surely even his past, her story placed with what he may remember as holy. Although they both appear middle-aged, there is something fresh in their union. In the beaming sun, *Anne*'s golden wood shimmers like syrup and the captain's gray beard is shimmering, too. Together they appear as a wish, a promising couple.

A therapist once suggested to me that every serious partnership begins with a wish that each partner harbors, a wish of what they each expect to gain from their union. She said often the partners are not even aware of the wish within themselves, and more often than not, the wish is not the same for each of them. She had suggested that my husband and I revisit our launching in order to reveal our initial secret wish to ourselves, and then to one another. At first, I couldn't imagine I had a wish, but all I needed to do was pop my shell and find it lying there, as shiny as a pearl. *I wish for you to take me beyond these hills.*

I wonder if beginning with a wish is true of men and their adored boats. And if so, does the wish exist at the launching as it does with lovers? Or is it instilled by the preparation and polishing and maintaining, or could it be that it will be born at sea, while waves toss them about and winds howl? I wish for you to save me. Or might the sailor's wish surface on the most beautiful of days? I wish for you to free me. I wish for you to calm me. I wish for you to take me beyond these hills. And could these be the wishes that we all harbor at one time or another, be it for Lord or lover, child or mother, boat or island?

Slowly crossing the deck from the scuttle, Ahab leaned over the side and watched how his shadow in the water sank and sank to his gaze, the more and more that he strove to pierce the profundity; but the lovely aromas in that enchanted air did at least seem to dispel, for a moment, the cantankerous thing in his soul.

And if once in a while we are to visit the wish for our intimate relationships, then perhaps once in a while we should visit the original wish for ourselves, finding that which is tucked away deep within our shell.

Feeling the warm sun beam down on my face and neck, on my bare legs and feet, listening to the lapping water and breathing the clear musky air, I realize I want to know what my original wish was for myself. Know I must, because although the air is rich enough to make me feel cleansed, my soul is often cantankerous too. Beneath the silky heat, I am empty without my sense of wonder. Even the cormorant will not look at me. Even he flies away and turns to sky.

two

The hauling truck starts up, making it impossible to hear what the men circling *Anne of Castine* might be saying, but I see their gentle gestures, and then over a lull in the truck's motor, the boat owner shouts, "We do it because we love it."

We do it because we love it.

What is it they do because they love?

Is he speaking of all men? Do they enter into a partnership with an unspoken wish, happy to do whatever it takes to keep things running smoothly because of love or duty? Or once aboard, do they simply accept life with all its profundity and causality, happy for the occasional lovely aromas in the enchanted air?

The truck backs up and its powerful hydraulics lower *Anne of Castine*, ME 2702A. She slides into the Bagaduce River like a strong sea serpent, her bow arched, her stern looking dangerously low to the water as she slips off the trailer. I suspect this is part of her playfulness. This is the way she teases her captain, part of her flirtation, her alerting him to her frisky details while whispering, *Know me.*

Anne is not the sleek serpent of the Garden of Eden or Basilisk or Draco, that serpent dragon who forever chases Ursa Major and Minor. Instead, she is reminiscent of a piece of blue pottery that Georgia recently made for me. It is a rendition of the Loch Ness Monster, four or five inches long with a flat shiny back and stretching neck and a gentle small head. Her outer coat is such a glistening and iridescent blue that you believe if you touch her, your fingers will be wetted. Beneath the blue is the reddest of ancient pottery, the red of the Prince Edward Island beaches that stained my feet when on holiday as a child. Nessie sits on the sail loft desk as if floating. Running my fingers over her, she becomes an undulating wave, cool and moving. When Georgia gave her to me, she said, "Mommy, Nessie is completely free. It doesn't matter to her what people think."

Georgia is thirteen and like my mother, she knows a lot of myths and tales. She has taught me about Draco and Basilisk and Nagini and Orky and the Massachusetts Bay Serpent, but she chose the Loch Ness Monster to methodically replicate. Nessie, who cruises freely, has remained in Georgia's memory for as long as she can remember, allowing her to replicate purely from recollection.

"Recollection of what?" I once asked her. "What is your first memory of Nessie?"

I wanted to know if there was an original love affair, a spark, but Georgia could not pinpoint her first memory of Nessie. I have since asked a number of her friends who also adore the primitive monster, and none are able to recall their introduction. For them, she has simply been. Always. Living in them.

"What part of your body does she inhabit?" I asked Georgia.

"Sometimes all around me, and sometimes in my heart, with a rope connecting her to my mind."

Instantly I imagined Georgia on the shores of Loch Ness, using the rope between her heart and mind, casting it out to reel Nessie in. Surely this is what we all want—to capture our most beloved myths and mysteries. But then what? Would that be too much truth, just as it was for Ahab when he finally caught Moby-Dick? If when we learn of something wild and spellbinding and thus far unattainable, it lives in us forever, becoming attainable in the most glorious way, in its eternal now, roped between our hearts and minds, then why must we reel it in? Why must we look into its eyes or have it look into ours? Why must we tame or caress or ride or possess it?

Georgia did not shape Nessie while looking at photos in *National Geographic* or remembering an evening watching a Loch Ness documentary, or by standing at the Loch Ness shore. She created Nessie from what lives within. Apparently with no beginning and never-ending, free and wild, known forever in her mind, maybe even part of her DNA. If studies now say there is a God gene, can a wonder gene be far behind? Or are they one and the same? And if it is part of our DNA to be full of wonder or to worship, why do some like me lose it? Will a black cormorant make me see again? Or even a flock of common seagulls? Will my eyes be opened by the fluttering of their wings, by the prodigy of plumage?

I suspect it is not because Nessie is wild and free that Georgia wanted to replicate her, but because Nessie doesn't care what people think. "She doesn't even care if people believe she exists," Georgia once said, her almond-shaped eyes looking amazed, as if they beheld a vital message.

Had I been caring too much? Trying too hard to keep up with this world? Had the wrong desires lulled me? Always looking for that captivating story to tell and then depleting my joy with countless retellings.

"Oh, Georgia," I said, having learned yet another thing from this child who surely has no beginning and no end. "That's the best, isn't it? To not care if people even believe we exist."

Maybe when we stop caring what others think, we find our true selves, our authenticity, our freedom. Maybe that is what some men find aboard boats while listening to the wind. That is their wish at launching: to be free, to be still and listen, to breathe deeply. Surely, that is what my father found while cruising. Once while walking with him in the cold November woods as a child, he made me stop and listen, hold very still. When I looked up, my steamy breath rose and mixed with his. Up high, the treetops made a wooing, washing, weeing sound.

"That is the great *wee* of pine and spruce," Dad said, touching the top of my wool hat with both of his hands, as if to seal the sound in. Listening, I felt a powerful yet beautiful sound. It smelled of melting river ice and blew through me like an essential and elemental message.

Know me.

Henry Beston said the three great elemental sounds in nature are the sound of wind in a primeval wood, the sound of rain, and the sound of the outer ocean when it crashes against a beach. I suppose the fourth element—fire—has its own powerful sound, but fortunately, few of us will ever hear it. It's easy to imagine, though, the snapping and thundering of fire as you race to escape it, as haunting an image as the resurrection of a frozen hummingbird is reassuring.

I see something of Nessie in *Anne of Castine* and something of *Anne of Castine* in Nessie. Despite their witnesses and admirers, the tourists and photographers, they move with their own beauty, solid yet sleek, confident yet whimsical, and there is original character to both—something that causes the admirers to come close, yet also to stay back. Of course, this is what I want for Georgia. This is what I want for both of my daughters. I want the world to notice their originality, to see what I see, but I don't want them to care if people believe they exist or not. And I never want them to be touched unnecessarily.

Kenny and Ted are now on the side dock holding *Anne's* lines and pulling her along to the front dock, which sits parallel to the shore. She is like a giant pull toy, her owner standing so still in the belly of her, that he could easily be a toy, too, placed there to make a scene more believable. But this is not the Disneyland that my daughters and I visited with its plastic fish hanging on strings around the submerged submarine, or the floating boats we boarded to tour that eerie dark cave while viewless children sang "It's a small world after all." This is real—the authentic life of a Maine village—as authentic and pure as children playing hopscotch in front of the corner store or collecting starfish and blue mussels from the pilings beneath the town dock.

"Listen, listen to sea," my five-year-old Phoebe says when we are stretched out on the town dock. She lies still with her ear on the worn, warm planks, her lush brown eyes blinking.

"What do you hear?" I ask.

"I hear the whole world."

"What does it sound like?"

"Like *weeeee*."

The great *wee* of the sea.

Kenny and Ted tie *Anne* and she is obedient, hugging the dock without getting too close, without scratching her sides. She pulses on the water, every bit alive and breathing, every bit of her potential showing, but no need to be showing off just yet, no need to let the world know that she even exists.

"My dad built her forty-five years ago," Kenny says.

Forty-five years ago.

I am smitten, my breath held.

Anne of Castine is the same age as I am.

I want to rush the dock the way young girls rush the stage at concerts. I want a backstage pass. I want to know where *Anne* was built and I want to know about Kenny's father. I want to become one of the faithful bystanders to *Anne*'s story, a witness, an admirer, a pathetic helper that Kenny shoos away, one who couldn't possibly understand the rules of launching. Could it be that *Anne* was conceived and built right here in Castine, and that her sails were made in the very sail loft that I am now occupying?

Kenny steps aboard *Anne* and her owner's stance instantly becomes less relaxed and a little guarded. This is the boatyard dance, the dance of owner and caretaker, reminding me of those polite cartoon chipmunks, Chip and Dale, but soon the men find their places. The owner stands near the bow and Kenny moves to the hatch and disappears.

The bilge pump starts, zippy and low-sounding, almost sonic, not like any boat I've ever heard, but maybe like Draco rushing through the sky or Nessie cruising Loch Ness. The witnesses gather closer, knowing that she will leave soon, knowing the sight of her will become memory—*Nice one, nice one, nice one.* Later, staring at the scarred lines on their palms, none will remember at what point the love affair began. She is simply now part of their DNA, living within.

The men lean on the pier's railing, looking down, a bird's-eye view. They are attentive and quiet, as if *Anne*'s sonic sound is calling them, hypnotizing them, soothing them, no less than an ancient hymn promising redemption:

Your company's sweet, your union dear;
Your words delightful to my ear,
Yet when I see that we must part,
You draw like cords around my heart.

Another man appears on the dock, older but strong-looking, with thick shoulders and thick white hair. He sits down at a nearby picnic table and then opens his newspaper. The subtle sonics seem to massage his broad shoulders, which slowly give way as he reads. His relaxation is similar to what the owner began to show once aboard *Anne*, similar to the contentment that some men show when a beautiful woman suns herself nearby. They don't need to stare, or yoo-hoo, or even glance, because they have memorized their *Anne* and she is safely tied between their hearts and minds. The one present simply serves to remind them of the eternal one, the elemental one, the essential one, the one who long ago whispered, *Know me.*

I suppose the *Anne* of some men's hearts is often memory turned to myth or myth turned to memory, all in his past and holy. Now, it is enough for him to know that she was once near, enough to know that she simply existed, or existed simply. They conjure her the same way Georgia and her friends conjure Nessie. And mature men remember the wonder of her, without the audacious telling and retelling.

Anne's bilge pump winds down and is silent—leaving the sounds of seagulls careening and calling—and beneath, the *weeeee* of the sea.

———

At Dennett's restaurant, which aligns itself with the west wall of the sail loft, tables and chairs thump as they are unstacked and arranged for lunch on the deck. On the town landing, an occasional vehicle parks, doors opening and shutting as passengers get out, and then stroll about the pier. A local man circles his bike around the parking lot. He appears several times a day, his bike seat set unusually high for his height. His wiry hair is gray and off the bike he has a limp, but on it, he powerfully and playfully circles the parking lot, a scene so much like one Fellini might create that I imagine circus music and begin to expect the unexpected.

Two dinghies coast by, buzzing like dragonflies, leaving a wake that is shallow and linear, and then it fades. Where do the wakes go? Do they continue waking until they reach the bottom of the sea? And is that why when diving, one finds the shapes of waves on the sea's sandy floor? If not, how deep can a wave go? It is said that abysmal waves caused the demise of the *Edmund Fitzgerald*, the swells of Lake Superior dipping the great ship down to rocks forty feet below. Perhaps the seagulls tried to warn them, but the sailors thought them only begging. Drowning in the cold sea, might the sailors have reached up and begged to the seagulls' prodigy of plumage? *Help me.*

A couple row out in a wooden dory reminiscent of another time, the oars making a gentle splash, their faces hidden by wide-brim canvas hats that are bleached and crinkled from years in the sun. The islands across the bay, Holbrook and Nautilus and Grays, are lush mounds, going on like a great serpent themselves, as linear as a long wave, stretching rather than dipping. The islands are made up of green: the blue-green of spruce, the light green of white pine, and meadow-green groves of oak over low-lying, dark green shrubbery—Elysian Fields—an orderly vision of paradise, landscaped naturally by the winds and waves. A park that Olmsted could only have designed in his dreams: a secret garden having reached its balance and harmony, its climax growth, a unique and perfect example of forest progression. What admiration my father would have had for this respected land. How sad he was when the big forestry companies started clear-cutting great chunks of the Canadian forests. He mourned the distant bald hills as if they were dear friends forever changed by a battle. It was while looking at one of these decimated hills that he said, *I don't believe in war. I don't believe in the greed of wiping anything out.* It was a broad and new definition of war for me, something I still ponder.

Looking across the harbor to the islands, one can easily imagine the empty fields before it all began, appearing as waves. Even now with lush growth, the islands seem to gently undulate—the time lapse easily envisioned—saplings spending their youth shaded by older trees while growing toward dappled sunlight, where they in turn form the canopy for future saplings.

TERROIR: the combination of terrain, weather, and culture. The culture being the Maine people, who for the most part have left the islands alone, allowing seeds to take, saplings to grow, canopies to expand, and climax growth to be achieved—the very thing we all want for our saplings, our children, one of the reasons that my husband and I chose Maine. It is said to be a state with one of the most stable cultures in the country, thus less development taking the place of forest and farmland and islands, permanently destroying the natural sight line. Here, the young are claimed by the land and sea early. Our daughters are testament to that, constantly begging us not to put them in the car, not to cross the causeway, not to take them off neck unnecessarily. Here, they have become enveloped by nature's canopy and the canopy of the locals watching over them. Here, they are one with the terroir.

Some might see parts of Maine as too stable or static, but it is said that it allows the climax growth to nurse its young better than other changing environments, where children are rushed from place to place or sit in curtained rooms watching cartoons and *The Price Is Right*, never to wade a stream or catch a pollywog in a jar. Edward Hoagland wrote, "If you wait until your mature years to get to know a patch of countryside thoroughly or intimately, your responses may be generic, not specific—just curiosity and good intentions—and you will wind up going in for golf and tennis and power mowers, bypassing nature, instead."

I suspect for the children sitting in commuting cars and curtained rooms, the price has not been right. It has been far too high for them, and for us, as well. How can we expect them to care about the natural world when they have barely experienced it? What pollywog will they ever consider worth saving, when they have not felt the silky life of its beating heart upon their palm?

Castine Harbor is waking up, moving from the time that was so still, so full of grace—the time which allowed me and a few others to witness an early launch. Now, the morning will be hyphenated with activity. By lunchtime, there will be a constant buzz of cars and trucks coming and going, running children laughing, dogs barking, and rock music playing at Dennett's. *Where do I go now, where do I go now, where do I go from here?*

A few motorboats will speed out to the open sea and sails will flap in the breeze that almost always comes by noon, and there will be the glorious greasy smell of fried clams and scallops, rich enough in the salty, breezy air to make you hungry even if you are not, and smelling convincingly good for you even if they are not. This is a morning in Maine, aptly portrayed by McCloskey and White and Jewett. Even so, this morning in Maine somehow feels uniquely mine. In the future, I may choose to see it as my evocation, my awakening, all shaping and gathering as if it had always been a wish within. Someday, these moments may be impossible to distinguish between memory and myth. Yet, it will likely be etched deeply in my palms. All taking place before seven a.m. on this Saturday, June 12, in a sail loft on the Bagaduce River, which keeps time with the sea, and the combination of salty air and simple sights and sounds is beautiful enough for me to suddenly consider all in my past holy and for the first time, perhaps all in my future, here.

Might I stay forever?

Any other morning might have been too wet or foggy, any other morning I might not have chanced here at the same time as *Anne of Castine* ME 2702A. And had it not been for a chance meeting with the owners of this sail loft one cold May day, I might not have had the good fortune of renting it for the summer. Even if I had walked Max longer this morning, out to Dyce's Head and the lighthouse on the southern point as I had planned, arriving thirty minutes later, with *Anne of Castine* already tucked to the outer dock, her story might not have been as compelling. Pretty, yes, but maybe not enough to captivate me, no zippy bilge running, no playful launch, no men gathering, no proclamation, *We do it because we love it.*

Inside, I sit in the wicker rocking chair near the window, a chair that is an exact replica of one from the summer rooms of my childhood home. Other people are on the dock now, looking down at *Anne of Castine*. The few are becoming more, and as if this is a signal for Kenny Eaton that things are getting too crowded, he walks up the ramp with his schoolboy jaunt that is quick and forward-racing. If he does stop, he will lift one leg and rest it on a ledge or rock or old lobster trap. It seems that he does this to relieve some sort of pain in his lower back. Maybe his sciatic nerve gives him trouble. Often, late in the day, I see him limping. Still, for the most part Kenny is always moving, his legs racing ahead of his apparent pain, carrying his thick stout frame, his life-ring belly, his tanned muscular arms that are always slightly bent and held from his body, ready, conjuring pictures of youthful fistfights and dance-hall brawls and of him, Kenny, almost always winning.

His face is ruddy and he often has uncombed hair which most will remember as white, but is really copper, not shiny but the dull of a bronze sundial that has been in the sun for years. His hair is white only in memory. Often when incoming sailors seek the owner of the boatyard, even the locals will say, Look for the guy with the white hair.

All the senior men at Eaton's Boatyard have hair that is remembered as white—Kenny and Sir Ted and Berkie—as if it is part of their *modus operandi*, one safely mistaken for the other, a God-given blessing in the swing of hot summer when people want everything done yesterday. Couldn't have been me you talked to. Musta been one of the others. Yes sa'r.

A ghost of chance, a ghost of possibility.

If one catches Kenny at the Variety before six a.m., sitting at one of the six counter stools and talking to the owners about the recent sighting of a deer in the village, or a late-night car crash on Route 166, they will see his hair wet and slicked back, his blue eyes crisp, his tanned and wrinkled face still boyishly handsome. I have come to think of each of those wrinkles as a survival story that he could tell. Some from myth, some from memory, all hauled and neatly tied within his seaman's chest.

Kenny has no hat, no sunglasses, no cell phone, no Day-Timer, no e-mail. Maybe he has tried some of these accessories, but has tired of them just as

I have tired of mine. Still, I suspect that he has never owned any. He has remained gadget-free. He is simply Kenny Eaton moving forward, unadorned, his late night limp more determined than crippled, his pace more boy than man, his way more wild than tame. He communicates in a husky voice with quick clipped sentences, sometimes gravelly hollering and hand signaling, and sometimes blasting swearing, as dark as the smoke from his unserviced and overused truck. When he turns angry, his voice becomes high enough to cut through fog.

Racing up the dock's ramp, Kenny nods to the older man reading his newspaper at the picnic table, the one that by loving one *Anne*, has admired many, and asks while still moving, "Been out to ya' boat yet?"

Without looking up from his newspaper, the man says, "Today."

"You saw where I moored her, then?"

The man simply nods, which is enough for Kenny, who is still moving forward as one of the more recently arrived men drifts toward him. Before the man speaks, Kenny hollers out, "C'mon, let's get'cha boat in the wat'ah."

The man stops short as if an impromptu launching couldn't possibly work. His long hands hang down. Up close, his fingernails would be as clipped and neat as a suburban hedge, his teeth gleaming and bleached from whitening chemicals, his speech cautious and measured. Yet from a distance, his tumbling thoughts are visible, the morning list vibrating in his head and building a case against launching the boat now. Maybe one o'clock would be better, after lunch when he's checked some things off that list, when he's had a chance to discuss the launching with his wife or girlfriend, maybe rearrange their plans. Not because he is weak or henpecked, but because he is loyal to his Day-Timer, and that keeps him ever faithful to his day. He possesses no natural boat-wrangling instinct. He is a man of well-laid plans.

"C'mon," Kenny says, opening the door to his battered red half-ton, the bed loaded down with anchors and tattered ropes. "I got a million things to do today. Stop ya' frettin'."

The man climbs into the truck, the to-do list suddenly gone—washed like salt from sea rocks by a convincing tide—rising, splashing, washing—and then thundering away. Maybe all men's beds are loaded down with anchors and ropes, tied conditionally to the to-do list for approval or temporary redemption. Maybe all men wait for that goading friend, the strong one that they can hitch their dreams to and be gone.

The man is smiling now, his boomerang-arm resting easy on the open window as Kenny wheels the truck around, heading back to the boatyard, zooming past the sail loft and Dennett's restaurant to the crowded corner, which is Eaton's Boatyard. Clearly, another city boy has been bullied by the untamed and is all the happier for it. Maybe it's unfair to say *city boy*. Maybe he is from a nice suburb of Washington or Connecticut, up for the weekend or a few weeks, but whatever time he has spent here, it has not been enough to learn the rhythm of chance, which is to say when a Castinian says *C'mon*, you should go. These are the opportunities, the payoff for the harsh winters. Most locals are not good with the prearranged. It interrupts their strut. To them arrangements are for visitors or summer people or newcomers and those who go for golf and tennis.

Castinians are experts at chance, and I—after having left my own *la-di-dah* suburb south of Boston for this small coastal village—am finally beginning to learn the rules of chance, and daresay I am happier for it. What freedom for the day to lead me rather than I lead it, my ear pressed to the town dock, listening unrushed with my daughters to the *wee* of the sea.

By chance last week, I boated out to Grays Island with the caretaker of its summer cottage. Native David Hatch and his wife Susie both grew up in Castine and have watched the changes over the years, some good and some bad. Still they remain gracious to newcomers. There was a time whenever my younger daughter met David on the sidewalk, she grabbed his hand and kissed it, as if she understood how much he as a local was sharing with her.

On my third day at the sail loft, David stopped by to make sure everything was okay. He is the caretaker of it as well. I told him how lucky I felt to have rented it for the summer.

"Suits you," he grinned, and then said he was boating two plumbers out to Grays Island, and asked if I wanted to come along.

For the shortest second, what I had planned reeled like a snake, but as if to rush from a recurring bad habit, I grabbed my scarf and followed him to the dock. Even though he has the to-do list of a city boy, he once invited me to be a passenger on the back of his Harley, where if he hadn't been impromptu, he would have simply waved and passed me by. Too much to do today. Instead, by chance, I have been cruising, and have the small burn scar on my ankle from the motorbike's exhaust pipe as a reminder. *Nice one, nice one, nice one.*

Stepping into the Whaler, David introduced me to the plumbers. One said hello, the other nodded without looking my way. Boating across the bright bay, they remained quiet, facing forward, their chins held high like seabirds.

While the men worked inside the cottage, I wandered about the island, which is a mound of rock and moss and low bush juniper. If I had been alone, I would have lain down on the warm sandy beach that curves around the southeast side, face to the sun, listening to the seagull that careened above, the orange dot on the underside of her beak lighting up like a spot of fire, the very spot that tells her offspring, *I am your mother, accept this food.* I would have lain very still, my eyes following that dot of fire, cradled by an island as if by the palm of God.

Leaving the island, we passed David's son's moored bait-dock. When researching lobstering for a novel, I had accompanied Josh on a few trips, always stopping to retrieve the rotting smelly pails of chum that are stored in buckets in a hatch below the dock. If the wind is right, the oily stench can take your breath away. It is the epitome of putrefaction. Once on another fishing friend's boat, a gag-inducing whiff of it combined with rough seas left me retching over the stern. My friend grabbed a sheet of plastic from the cabin and covered the bait, but the rotting smell still wafted about as apparent as an oily film on the surface of the sea.

I returned from my trip to Grays Island with my pockets full of periwinkles and a gray rock shaped like a crowded heart. It lies on the sail loft desk, reminding me of an island not far away, an island made of rocks and moss where a mother flies the sky. If the Great Creator can make an insect from sand, then how simple this bird must have been, how easy the shaping of an orange dotted beak.

Now, I want nothing more than to know everything about *Anne of Castine*, ME 2702A, my newfound sister and desired twin, but it is best not to track Kenny down. What I learn of *Anne* will come by chance. Maybe when Kenny is sitting next to me at the Variety, eating his two barely cooked boiled eggs from a bowl, maybe I'll take a chance and ask. I picture him dipping his butter-soaked toast in the runny eggs, slurping his coffee, chewing while juggling several conversations with other patrons, or maybe I'll choose another time. The thing about Kenny is he often runs while he eats, too. Even when sitting, he is idling and ready for takeoff. Maybe I'll want to ask about *Anne*, but Kenny will have his walls up, treating me like a newcomer to keep me in my place as he sometimes does, or maybe it will be too communal, a time when others might join in with their own stories of *Anne*, their wrinkles full of memories, too. Although it will be tempting, it will lack the intimacy I desire with *Anne* the first time out, no different than what her owner obviously craves at her launching.

Maybe I'll hear about *Anne* while taking the shortcut back home through the boatyard. Kenny will be moving from one weathered building to another, his boots with orange laces loosely laced—moving through the old buoys and lobster traps, the ropes and empty cans of boat paint, the cultch, as the local poet Philip Booth so aptly called it—and Kenny will slow down just a bit, maybe to say he wishes his daughter would lease me her inherited 1949 lobster boat for the summer—something I asked him about last summer—or maybe to ask how I like slumming it near the boatyard. If his walk is slow enough, I may chance to say, Kenny, what can you tell me about *Anne of Castine*?

And he may say, Why—do you want to lease her, too? And I will say, No, I just want to know her.

Or maybe I won't have to keep up with Kenny. Maybe he'll stop and rest that tired leg on a buoy or broken wooden trap, squinting his sky-blue eyes while his face opens up to the sun, telling me something of *Anne*, but not everything, because men like Kenny don't stop for long, and boats like *Anne* only reveal themselves over time.

three

$\mathcal{B}$y chance my husband Bill and I found Castine, and by chance, I have rented the sail loft for the summer as my writing studio. It has been twelve days since I turned the key and entered a small, ship-like building, facing a wall of twenty-four molten windows that magnify the harbor. Instantly, I was ushered into another time, looking out the stern of a frigate, nose to port, the wide, long, oiled-rich boards stretching around me, boards the color of broken sea pottery and the ruddy red beaches of Prince Edward Island.

Sepia once described the color of octopus ink on paper, and sepia is the color that permeates the sail loft. The ceiling is dropped low like a canopy and everything smells of burnt molasses. The smoke from many wood fires has claimed a portion of the oxygen, but I am more than willing to be without my full breath, to be held in reverence for this place, which I have long admired, but only dreamed of inhabiting.

Instantly I knew that over the summer I would become familiar with its seasoned white pine, and the constant changing of the tides beneath its pilings, that I would touch and admire every part of the old building and in the end, no doubt cherish and enjoy it above all others. Even the rambling ancestral home of my childhood will probably not compare, its deep line in my palm fading and making way for the sail loft.

On the wall near the door is a black-and-white photograph of a white-bearded man. He is wearing a canvas bibbed apron over a white shirt and he is sitting on wrinkled sheets of sailcloth. The look in his eyes is distant, but also resigned. Resigned to what? The hard job of making sails, or is he far from home and homesick? I like to think that he is Italian, because while researching my last novel, I discovered that Italians came to the nearby coastal islands to mine granite, or perhaps he sailed from much farther away, and his tired-looking eyes represent distance. My daughters and I call him the sail loft man. When I enter in the early mornings, I touch his face as if I am touching the worn feet of that marbled saint inside the Vatican's entrance. *Help me to write well today.*

To the left of the sail loft's entrance is a small galley kitchen with aging yet functioning appliances. A tiny bathroom tucked behind the kitchen has a noisy electric heater and an employee's time clock that ticks and clicks every three minutes. To the right of the door are a large trunk and two single built-in beds. Above one bed hang the remnants of several old posters, all advertising a play titled *The Wages of Sin.* The posters are tattered the way I suppose most sins appear once one wearies of them.

Halfway between the entrance and the opposite wall of windows is a desk with a battered captain's chair. On the desk is a piece of white coral shaped like a man's reaching hand, and when I arrived, there was a small alarm clock, but I slipped it inside the desk drawer, feeling there was no need to live in *chronos* here.

The desk is snug against a Victorian sofa covered with tea-stained linen. Placed before the windows and the un-railed deck beyond, the sofa is as inviting as the gentle slope of a horse's back. From it, the sight line is uninterrupted, and often in the early mornings, a mist hovers over a black moored lobster boat and a yellow sailboat, christened *Caution.* The mist is gauzy up close, but so dense farther out that the southerly islands of Holbrook and Nautilus and Grays are wrapped in a white as solid as wedding paper. Someone looking at the mist for the first time wouldn't know the islands existed. They'd simply imagine the sea going on forever.

In the center of the sail loft and to the left is a long table with benches that suggest a monastery, but when my seaworthy French brother-in-law visited last week, he said the table was probably built for a ship.

"Why do you think that?" I asked.

"The square-braced base suggests anchoring," he said, "something to keep the table from moving when the seas turned rough."

Rubbing the table, I was reminded of a favorite oak bowl, salvaged from the wood of an old ship and polished to a smooth pockmarked surface. Wood that when touched has the power to release its history. I envisioned the *Edmund Fitzgerald* sinking on Lake Superior, imagining myself as a trapped sailor, and then shivered.

"Are you okay?" my brother-in-law asked.

Yes," I said. "I was just thinking."

Was I thinking or imagining or remembering? Had rubbing the table conjured a dream or a memory born from wood? Had I left *chronos* for *kairos*, where music can float forever and the echoes of the galaxies being born can still be heard? How could anyone forget those astronauts listening to nostalgic music being played in their spaceship? When they radioed NASA to thank them, NASA said they were not sending music. Months of research revealed that they had heard a radio program that had aired in the 1930s. This story and my own shivering inspired me to later research the history of the *Edmund Fitzgerald*, revealing no record of a woman aboard, only men and a cat named Simon. I suppose there could have been a lovesick stowaway or a captured mermaid. Maybe all captains did not resist the rockbound sirens singing as Odysseus did, instructing his crew to fill their ears with wax and tie him to the mast, so he might listen to the haunting voices, yet resist steering the ship dangerously close to the rocks.

Countless mermaid sightings have been recorded, creatures with long hair swimming beside great ships. When they turn to swim on their backs, they reveal the torso of a woman, full breasts and curving hips pouring down into an iridescent supple fin. Is this what sailors really witnessed, or did their lonely desire create an image powerful enough to be real? Some predict it was only manatees swimming beside the great ships, but who are they to say? They were not there.

On the wall behind the long table are colorful peeling movie posters from the early 1900s. The owners of the sail loft said the owner before them had tried to remove the posters but found it impossible, so they remain in tattered pieces. They appear to have been burnt, and now only smoky remnants remain. If you squint, the tatters take on the manifestation of marble or granite, a patina that seems capable of remaining forever. The owners warned me that pieces of the posters would drop from time to time, and asked me to preserve them in a basket near the kitchen, but so far not a single remnant has fallen. The posters have remained as undisturbed as the sea nymph's sleeping shells beneath the sail loft. Even when the winds blow through, making papers on the desk flutter, nothing has fallen away.

Perhaps my half-held breath of reverie has slowed time. And maybe that is what happened when I held still in front of the barracuda long ago. Time slowed. It is said that nothing in all creation is so like God as stillness. If that is the case, maybe by being still I was not feeling the wonder of a barracuda, but the wonder of creation. And what about those astronauts admiring the heavens as the magical soundtrack played? What place had they entered? And what wonder was being bestowed upon them? And if we can enter a place of wonder, can we also enter a place of warning, be it through a dream or a vision?

On one poster, a man's face has been ripped away with visible force—the way a disgruntled woman might destroy a lover's picture—and only a strip of printing remains. I rub my fingers over the teal-blue letters, wondering how the color has stayed so crisp and clear, the blue not only of Caribbean seas, but of my dear mother's eyes. How I long for them. It has been a year since her heart took its final beat, my own heart instantly slowing to a mourning pace. In my chest, it is as heavy as a bear cub. How I missed her wise reassurances, her object lessons, and fables.

Nearby, there is a large golden-framed portrait of a fair-haired boy who I instantly disliked. Perhaps it is his weak shoulders or smug smile, with tinges of contempt. Is he mocking me? Next to the portrait is the skull of a large cow, smooth white hollow bone. The two make a lovely juxtaposition, the black holes of the cow's missing eyes and the boy's cold blue stare. Maybe in a spoiled rage the boy ordered the slaughtering of the cow and now the ghost of the cow hangs with him. Maybe this is what happens—the ghosts of our mistakes hang like etchings on the wall of our consciousness.

Beyond the table are three small, stacked weathered trunks. Sometimes the front of the middle one will drop down unexpectedly, revealing shelves piled with old photographs. I shut it without looking—not yet—even though I am tempted. It would be a mistake to take in the details of the sail loft too quickly. When my daughters visit me at work, they scurry through things like mice, making me nervous. Not only because they are not our things to scurry through—although the owners themselves are inquisitive, and I know would welcome their curiosity—but I am superstitious of too much being revealed too quickly. Like the peeling posters, every piece should fall in its own time, before the full picture can be glued back together.

The trunks are embraced by two gothic armchairs with faded scenes of courting lovers carved on their backs. Behind them is a steel eye screwed into the wall and used for stretching sails. I have found four others, making me envision the sail loft man's strong hands stretching and pulling the cloth, his palms bound in protective worn leather to keep the stitching needle from piercing his palm. Was it he who put up the movie posters, feeling lonely in this remote place? Was it he who lined up the several copies of the *Wages of Sin* poster so they hovered above him while he read or rested, while he slept and dreamed? And what demons did he wrestle? What music from long ago played in his head? What palm scars did he stare down at when he woke? And what were his two selves, his two sorrows?

With all the stitching he did, his grip must have been that of a strong lover's. I see the long-gone strength of his hands now preserved in the white coral resting on the desk, coral that I touch for luck, as often as his photograph. Now, when I see the coral weed growing in tidal pools around this peninsula, I am reminded of the sail loft man. Coral weed is the only seaweed that grows upright and resembles a waving hand. In it, I see his scarred palm with open fingers, waving.

A Franklin stove sits on a raised brick hearth on the southwest wall. In the early mornings, I often start a fire to take away the dampness. For hours the smell of oily creosote remains. If I close my eyes, I become a girl again, recalling the morning after a chimney fire in our living room fireplace. My defeated-looking mother was fanning the air with a folded newspaper, her forehead smudged with soot in the shape of a cross. The look on her face conjured up such sadness in me that I felt her defeat.

Behind the stove is a bricked-in arch that creates a mantel, which holds the white bust of a woman's face. She sits in profile and her chin is held proudly. She could be Roman, but I choose to think that she is Native American, since most of the sail loft's contents belonged to the previous owner, who wore large turquoise necklaces and his white hair pulled in a ponytail. Once on the steps of the Variety, he admired my long black hair and straight nose, and then we talked about the tribes of Maine. Before we parted, he asked me if I had Indian blood. I didn't know what to say. That part of my bloodline had only been mentioned in a teasing way, my brothers often saying that Mom had brought the wrong baby home from the hospital.

In the crowded maternity wing, she had shared her room with a woman from the nearby Maliseet Reservation. My brothers were so astute with their teasing that as a child, I often wondered about my other parents, my other siblings. Maybe that is where my restlessness originated, the feeling of having two selves. Once, when my father stopped by the reservation to visit his friend and the tribe's chief, Amos, I had everything I could do not to tear from the car and ask if my other self lived on the reservation. Did he know her? What was she like? Did she look more like my siblings than me?

On that day, Amos lit a cigarette and passed it to Dad. Indians in movies passed a peace pipe the same way. Amos's black Lab, Canuck, sat between them, panting, his coat gleaming like a velvet cloak, his pink tongue as plush-looking as a girl's slipper. I knew as always that Canuck would soon move to the side of our car, sniffing the wheels, and then my little brother Aubrey and I would reach out the side windows to pat him.

Near Amos, an overturned polished canoe rested on two sawhorses. My father stepped sideways and then rubbed his fingers over the golden sheen admiringly, even though he had warned us many times about the dangers of a canoe, how tippy they were. I suppose this fear stemmed from his general fear of water. Watching his children swim, he always stood at the shore as regal as a cormorant, carefully keeping us in his peripheral vision as he smoked and took in the vistas around him.

Still, on that day, it was easy to see he appreciated the gleaming canoe and Amos's care for it. Like the tiny reservation houses built by the government several years earlier, some of the canoes in other yards were now rotting and in disrepair. These same yards often had tied scrawny dogs, so depleted they never barked or even glanced up when our car passed. Yet Dad warned us that despite the dogs' laziness, they could still bite. Many dug holes like graves beneath themselves, and some even chewed through their ropes to escape, their abandoned tethers lying like snakes all summer long. Dad said more than once he had come across a feral mongrel while cruising in the woods. It was an image that took my breath away, while inspiring Mom to tell us several myths of wild dogs, my favorite being one of a black dog that wandered through cemeteries on stormy nights, protecting the dead from the Devil. She said the dog was called a *church grim*.

That day, Amos disappeared behind his house, and Dad glanced back at me. He was frowning and appeared worried. I thought maybe Amos, as the tribe's chief, had gone to retrieve some document, something that might prove my true identity, and my breath weighed heavy in my chest. Maybe my true history was about to be revealed and my life would be changed forever. Maybe I would have to leave my home and drift through tattered yards of dogs with their abandoned ropes that lay like the shed skins of snakes.

Aubrey must have read my mind. He reached over the backseat and patted my shoulder.

"Don't you think Dad looks like an Indian, too?"

Too. The word came from him like a dove's mourning call. He, too, had been witness to my brothers' teasing, and I suppose if it were true, he did not want me to be exchanged for the unknown sister, nor would I have wanted to leave him. He was my confidant, my first tethered friend, and I his. Only a year and nine months between us, we had bonded like doves nestled on a branch.

Canuck came to the side of the car. We reached out and patted his black and sun-warmed coat. He smelled of river water, fresh and running, and when I recall that smell now, I remember it as also having the unsullied smell of spring sap dripping from a maple tree.

Soon Amos returned with a large basket of fiddleheads and the heaviness in my chest collapsed. Dad bent over the wicker basket and admired the wet green ferns glistening in the sun. We knew that Amos had paddled out to one of the river islands for the fiddleheads, and that Canuck had swum along beside the canoe. Amos always got the first fiddleheads of the season, just as he got the first perch and trout, the first partridge and moose and deer. Peas and new potatoes appeared in his garden long before anyone else's, as if something in his large hands had cultivated earliness when he placed the seeds in the turned earth. Season after season, he shared his bounty with us.

As always, Dad took out his wallet, offering to pay Amos, but Amos shook his head, no. Back home, the fiddleheads would be served with a salmon caught from the Miramichi River. It was a taste we'd all learned to crave as the winter drifted behind us and the snow and ice melted and the river rose, the taste of new greens and salty fried salmon skin. It was our family's spring tonic.

After putting the basket in the trunk, Amos came to the window, reaching his large hand in to touch my head. His hand smelled of plowed earth and felt as cool as springwater in a shaded stream. He bent over and smiled at Aubrey in the backseat.

"Boy," he said, smiling as if *boy* were a word that always traveled on a wind within him. Amos's hair was long and shiny like Canuck's coat, and his white teeth gleamed like his dark eyes.

Girl, I longed for him to breathe, wondering if it too lived in him. *Girl* . . .

Leaving the reservation, a girl about my height ran to the edge of her yard. The tiny house behind her was still unfinished, yet it also appeared tattered, as if some part of it had been sped forward into old age while another part remained stunted in its inception. Pink insulation stuck out around the door and windows, resembling the innards of a salmon. A grimy lace curtain hung outside an unscreened window like the tattered train of a wedding dress. Thistles and purple violets grew wearily in the dirt where a green lawn should have been.

From a distance, the girl's body had appeared round like a baby's, and her face had a hint of the mongrel dog's, something undefined that looked even from afar like vague suffering, as vaporous as the communal burden of an uprooted tribe. Up close though, the girl's face appeared scarred, as if she had once stood in front of a great fire and had begun to melt, that feared elemental sound snapping and chasing her until she simply turned and faced it. Might she have heard the fire roaring, *girl?* Might that have been the reason that she turned?

Her thick black hair was short and her straight bangs, cut crooked. She stared at us passing, her small dark eyes glistening like an eerily moonlit sky. She seemed about my age. For a time, I wondered if she might be me.

"What's wrong with her?" I asked.

"*Hutlanee,*" Dad said.

I looked back at Aubrey. Neither of us knew the word. It was an Amos word, one of the many that Dad understood and sometimes used, one of the words they passed back and forth between them like a peace pipe. Yet it sounded enough like a swear word that I saw Aubrey practicing it under his breath. *Hutlanee.* Later, I would watch him running through the hayfield behind our house, a broken branch held high over his head like a spear. Again and again, he pointed and stretched the spear toward the sky. *Hutlanee, hutlanee, hutlanee,* he chanted.

Years later while reading a Native tale to my daughters, I learned the meaning of the word *hutlanee.* "Bad luck." By then, I had long ago identified the nature of the fire that had melted that young girl's face. Fetal alcohol syndrome. A searing liquid, catching her before she'd even had a chance to crawl or walk or run, its heat blasting her again and again in the tomb of a womb called Mother. At first, it probably only warmed her as she floated in its syrupy bath, making her chromosomes sticky. After, those chromosomes burst and bloated like glue. They should have smelled of sweet bursting sap, but they no doubt smelled of burnt sugar. How her baby fingers must have scratched at the sooty womb walls to escape. *Sooty womb walls, sooty womb walls*, the chant echoing through her like a tribal drumbeat.

Staring at her, it seemed that invisible hands were pulling her face apart. Her features were a struggle. Finally, learning the meaning of the word *hut-lanee*, I thought how luck or the lack of it in one's life could certainly be considered a condition, a sentence worthy of violently pounding a spear toward the heavens. I wished then for one of my mother's fables: a tale of a feral dog that protects a child in its mother's womb.

I imagined the girl's parents, old and staring at their palms with deep crevices shaped like clawing marks. Trying to remember their lives, their daughter, they hold their scarred palms to their faces and cry. Of course. On that little government-planned reservation, they could barely see the river down in a valley beyond them now, a meandering blue paradise they once owned and walked beside every day, their lodges only a stone's throw away from its lapping edge, a river that had since been dammed to make way for progress. Now they lived in small, unfinished houses that faced one another instead of the lush land and the seasoned hills and the waterway, day after day, as if staring into a smoky mirror. Nothing new under the sun. Tipping the white man's river to their lips, they too no doubt heard a primal war dance beating. Hopeful is how the hot liquor would have made them feel at first, but after too much drinking, they laid together, thrashing with impaired rhythm, their tethered yard dog listening and gnawing at its rope, wishing like them to be freed.

Maybe the woman's carved face on the mantel has no origin with Native Americans, just as I may not, and just as the sail loft man may not be Italian, but what sin is it to imagine, if some story is released? Surely, we cannot be punished for our own guided imagery. Or can we?

The bust is painted with a thick white paint. Obviously not the appropriate paint, for some of it has lifted and begun to crack away like ice lifting from a river's shore. Beneath it she is the color of damp peat. I imagine the sail loft man rescuing and then painting her, slapping the heavy brush to create a gauzy color at first, but coat by coat, layer by layer, the opaque became as thick as the wedding-paper fog that sometimes clings to the southerly islands.

A piece of her neck is broken away and there is a wide slash on the back of her head. The wood is spongy as if she were wet for a very long time. Had she floated on an open sea—had his hand reached down, snagging her with his coral strength to safety? And what goes through a man's heart when he finds the image of a woman at sea? Does he long to be closer to her as Odysseus did? And how much of her face was already that of a woman's when he found her, or was she simply a hunk of wood shaped from his desire, like a plump manatee turned into a mermaid by a sailor's desire?

Studying her, I am reminded of a clay mask that a sculptor did of my face—a long process of layering wet gauze, one thin strip upon the other—while my eyes remained closed, my lips parted for breathing. Beneath the cool mask, it was dark and tomblike. I thought of the Shroud of Turin, and how Christ's face was said to be a stain upon a cloth now. Countless prints and photographs of the Shroud reveal a sad human face, yet it is somehow flawless too. Studying these photographs, I always find the silence possessed within that gaze almost deafening, the same silence I felt in the gaze of the girl on the reservation. Is it the silent gaze of recognition or the gaze of instruction. *Know me*? Should we, as George Eliot suggested, die of that roar which lies on the other side of silence?

My mask reveals everything. A high forehead, feathery eyelashes, and wrinkles at the corners of my eyes, a straight nose, pores on my cheeks, an overbite, and a mole on my chin that my mother called a beauty mark. The mask was not created by desire, but duplicated exactly with patience, and she is as truthful as an X-ray. I despise her, even though I shouldn't. I could have been a girl born with a melted-looking face. The mask is my story unembellished, she is me laid bare, and she does not look as young as I often perceive myself to be.

On that fateful day last summer when Mom would die, I lifted my mask down from the linen closet. The rising sun had so much feverish heat that it simmered brownish syrup from the lilacs. I'd hidden the mask behind a stack of pillows as soon as I had returned home with it. A friend had done an etching of a sleeping woman's face surrounded with white goose feathers, and I thought of that etching as I hid the mask away, just as I thought of it when I retrieved it.

I knew that I was trying to retrieve some part of my younger self. Little did I know, I would conjure a banshee instead, a woman of the fairy mounds, a woman of any age that suited her, her wailing always signifying the death of a great person. After placing the mask on my dressing table, I painted her lips red, lining them first with a lip pencil to keep the color from bleeding. Yet even with painted lips, I didn't like her, although I wanted to—in the same way that I now wanted to like the portrait of the smug boy in the sail loft. Looking at the mask, I wanted to paint her jet black, all of her. A simple touch of red had not worked. She should be the opposite. Not white and laid bare, but black and mysterious. Cloaked. Yes, that was it.

I sat down on my bed, fully aware of the adrenaline pumping through my veins, fresh yet sticky like the tinged sap that seeped from the lilacs, sap that could eventually trap me like glue, as I contemplated another thing that day. A shrouding of sorts. And in the end, I would be no more successful than one trying to shroud the stench of rotting fish with a sheet of plastic. Some things are simply too penetrating to be covered and hidden.

Leaving to buy plants, I glanced back at my daughters in the garden. I waved and they waved before turning and resuming work on their fairy house.

For the slightest second, my heart pulled toward them as if the invisible knitting between us was shrinking. It was similar to a feeling that I had many years earlier on the morning when Mom had her first stroke. We had just a few days earlier celebrated her forty-ninth birthday. On her bed, she lay limp and gasping for air. A photo album was open beside her. For months, she had been researching her family tree. Yet the album was not opened to the distant relations, but instead to a black-and-white photograph of her mother holding her when she was a baby. It was the last one taken of them together. Sitting in the snow, her mother is holding her firmly, but also at a distance, as if she is rehearsing parting with her. Still, even with the distance between them, they appear woven together. My grandmother's eyes are closed and she has the look of satisfaction. She is wearing a dark coat and hat and her plump baby is in a sweater set. Never did we look at that photograph together that Mom didn't say in a pleased way, *My sweater set was red.* This comment always seemed incongruous to me. Why was she focusing on the color of her sweater set and not the sadness of their last image together?

Watching Mom on her bed as she struggled to breathe that morning, I knew that I was inextricably woven to her. The red weave of us tightened in my chest and the threat of her dying forced me to pray, promising to always be a good girl. Always. Just let our mother live.

Years later, I would read about the Stendhal syndrome in which Italians were affected physically when they viewed the Renaissance masterpieces for the first time, autobiography as nightmare, and I wondered then if that was what Mom had experienced while viewing her mother's photograph that morning, thus causing an artery in her own heart to shut. Was she struck and then immobilized by a memory woven into her DNA, was she somehow inextricably tethered to the memory of her own mother dying? Had she finally let her preoccupation with her red sweater set recede, focusing on the sadness instead? *Yet when I see that we must part, you draw like cords around my heart.*

My silly desire to shroud the bust in black was inspired by a letter from an old boyfriend—whimsical black script listing his reminiscences of me—saying that he would be passing through in a few months and would love to take me to lunch. For old times' sake. When the letter arrived several weeks earlier, the only word I saw was the word *love*. It bloated and hung like a sun-ripened strawberry, even though I knew Castine was always a detour. No one passed through unless by sea.

His writing was heavier than I recalled, as if he'd held his pen with a fierce hand. A hobbyist of handwriting analysis, I studied it for clues. On the envelope, his return address was writ large as if to represent a secret code with loops and twirls. There was no post office box number for me, just my name and town and postal code. I gathered he had done a bit of research to find me.

I had taken my time before mentioning it casually to my husband. "Go ahead and have lunch. It's not like you are going to run off with him," he said.

It's not?

At the time, two things seemed to be motivating me. Curiosity, and that written word, *love*. Of course, retrospect will reveal things to be more complicated, but in those moments, I endlessly entertained myself with questions. How had twenty-plus years changed him? What demons did he wrestle? What music from long ago played in his head? Was he sick or dying? What were his two loves? His two sorrows? Was I one love? One sorrow? Did I curl and tighten like a rope around his heart? *Girl* . . . or could he be attempting to bind me like the man's belt and the woman's tattered flip-flop that I had found lying on the beach? His written reminiscences had made me feel like a girl again, the one that wore her father's straw fedora, the one that fearlessly hitchhiked, the one that had once been kissed so long and tenderly by him that she saw her whole life before her. It appeared as inviting as an open field.

Of course, I suspected that his recollections were meant to serve as ignition, camouflaging the hunter's intention, but I was willing to ignore the risk behind the flame roaring, *girl*. His letter had included a photograph of a young me standing on the black bridge near home in faded blue jeans and a T-shirt, my long hair gleaming like the dark water that ran in the creek below. Instantly, I smelled tar and fresh cold creek water and lily of the valley and white-throated sparrows sang, *Oh, sweet Canada*.

He recalled how he first met me by picking me up hitchhiking after I had tired of my nightly run. He reminded me that it was November and that tiny snowflakes were whipping about in a fierce wind, and he wrote that when I got into his car, a cold confetti of snow followed me that took days to melt.

You chatted openly. You asked me a string of questions. And while I was driving you home, you made me pull into the driveway of a farm so the car's headlights picked up the silhouette of a deer hanging upside down in the doorway of a shed. Do you remember? The snow had stopped. The stiff carcass swayed in a howling wind. You said it was against the law to shoot a doe. Crimson blood pooled beneath her, her throat slit and dripping, and do you recall that you wanted me to cut the deer down?

Yes, I wanted you to retrieve a doe's life. I wanted to believe it was possible. And then I wanted the doe to grow velvet-looking horns. And then I wanted her to run once again.

I knew that if I allowed myself to be captured by him, that afterward, I would not be allowed to hang openly while someone begged for my rescue. We live in a world where women are still judged more harshly than men for their infidelities, as if female temptation is unnatural. Men will be men, but women will be labeled as harlots.

Still I reminisced about his strong jaw, his square white teeth, and skin so thin that the hidden places of him revealed powerful-looking veins, something that I had once considered to be his secret map. His skin that witnessed the sun always remained as tanned as russet leather both in winter and summer. I recalled how his gray eyes could sometimes look weary and hold a distant look just like the sail loft man's, and I began to wonder if that look had been a sign of his longing, or his resignation.

When I finally answered his invitation, I suggested that we meet at an outdoor cafe in a nearby fishing village. Now that date was a day away.

———

Near a gathering of blue irises at the garden center in Blue Hill, I leaned against a pile of railroad ties, feeling faint, which I surmised was from the bright white and suffocating heat. For a moment, my throat felt as it did when my mother had had her first stroke, as if the remnants of a dried and burnt nest had gathered there.

The tarry-smelling railroad ties were hot, too, as if a long racing train had just passed over them. It was then that a flock of tiny white butterflies descended, so many that they appeared as a summer snow whirling about. Snow that had miraculously never melted. I closed my eyes, listening for the butterflies' flapping wings to gather into sound, but there was nothing. How I longed for a flapping crescendo, like bedsheets in a convincing wind. How I longed for a beckoning sign.

The desire lulled me, but soon the image of the sheets parted and it was the train from my childhood that appeared, the one that my mother and I often took to visit loved ones. The train was moving away, along a track that entered a forest lit by white light. On the caboose stood a young woman whom I assumed to be me. She wore a straw fedora slanted on her head and she was waving. Her lips were painted red. For the shortest second, I thought I heard the faint rattle and chug of the train. Taking the train as a child with my mother was one of my favorite outings. Boarding the train with my hand in hers, I always felt that a new beginning awaited us. Not that I didn't love the life we had, but even then, I was sometimes restless and dreamt of running.

When I returned home, dazed from the hot garden center, the truck's bed loaded down with as many bushes and flowers as it would hold, Bill came to the open passenger window, his eyes worried and his lips downward. Immediately, I looked for our daughters. It occurred to me that I had not thought of them since leaving. I had thought of my old boyfriend instead. The girls stood in the back garden, hanging on to each other's hands, their faces as questioning as orphaned fairies. Why have you forsaken us?

The image of me waving from the train's caboose appeared and then I felt the weight of my selfish thoughts and the face of that young woman on the train became clear and I knew at once that it wasn't me, *chug, chug, chug,* but the sound of a fleeting heartbeat.

"Bill, it's Mom, isn't it?"

I hoped for his worried gaze to continue meeting mine, for him to say, It's another stroke, but he said nothing, and I knew that on the brightest and sweetest-smelling summer day thus far, or maybe ever, with white butterflies fluttering about like snow and lilac seeping their sap, she had left. My mother had boarded the train without me.

We understand death for the first time when he puts his hands on one whom we love. I knew this detonating feeling, this loss, had felt its full force when my father died six years earlier.

I tore from the truck, running in my calico skirt and flip-flops and sleeveless white blouse, the same summer outfit I'd often worn as a child, shaking my suddenly burning hands and saying, *no, no, no,* racing to my bedroom to call her, Wait, not yet, Mom. I'm not ready, not ready to be without your sweet smell, your robin's-egg-blue eyes, your caressing hands, and although I could never have put this into words then, although it would take months to realize, and the realization would be the impetus for my deepest depression thus far. I was not ready to be without her intent gaze, her intuition, her instructions, her prayers. Where would I end up without her? Where would my selfish musings take me? Hadn't I promised long ago to always be a good girl in exchange for her life? Had she slipped away to protect me from my own regret, or was God punishing me? Now instead of meeting an old boyfriend for lunch the following day, I would be planning her memorial service with my siblings.

The clay bust stared from my dressing table. Someone had smudged the red lipstick and her chin was smudged with tiny bloody fingerprints, filling the porous white, an inerasable stain that registered instantly as the smear of death. Not black, like one might expect, but red. The fresh bruising before the shrouding, the deceit, the doe hanging and sacrificed, my mother's final stroke, rupturing, bleeding, no more pleasing mention of her red sweater set.

What did it mean that on the day of her departure I had taken my tomb-like face down from the closet, painting the lips red as I contemplated disloyalty, luxuriated in the thought of it while daydreaming myself as a young beguiling girl, a young girl running toward an open field.

And which of my daughters had tried to wipe the lips clean, or had they done it together, hand in hand, wanting to wipe the brazen red away just as they will forever want to wipe away the smear of their grandmother's death. *Nannie.*

Mom could not be dead. I had just spoken to her the night before. She was excitedly waiting on my oldest brother George to visit the following day. He was salmon-fishing on the Miramichi, and then planning to visit her as he always did, with news of his catch and of the river, which had offered it up to him. And of course, she would prompt him by asking if the river was high or low, what about the blackflies, had they been bearable, and the cook's cooking? And which of his old school friends had gone along with him this time?

And then she had talked about family, repeating the word again and again like a message. *Family.* Of course. Where had my intuition been? Had I given myself over to a longing for my past and missed intuiting something of my present? Had my own guided imagery betrayed me? My foolish desire to feel young again.

Mom and I often dreamed the same dreams on the same nights. If she was ill, I dreamed it. If I were ill, she dreamed it. Why had a dream of her dying not availed itself to me? Why had I not known? What cave had I floated into? What ridiculous fake voices had lulled me? And why did she die on this day? Perhaps, because all her intuitions had remained true. She must have dreamed me drowning in my own sentimentality, the smell of its sweet rancidity alerting her. Maybe she died to rescue me, and now her death would serve as a lesson in justifiable sentiment. She had died while longings swirled in my head, flaunting and blinking the word *girl*.

I sifted through our last conversation for clues. She spoke of assisted living, as if she could endure it forever, if only they would get the name right.

"What *should* they call it?" I'd asked her.

"Well, they used to call them nursing homes," Mom said, "and before that they were called old folks' homes. That's the most accurate. Really, that's what is here. Old folks. Every one of us is worn out in one way or another. You can smell it, Deborah. You can smell the letting go of life."

I wanted to ask what it smelled like, the letting go of life. Did it have something of the sardines she so despised, or the putrefaction of bait, or maybe the sickly smell of too many blossoms, of sentimentality? Instead, we spoke of family.

I could not remember the phone number for the assisted-living facility, or the telephone numbers for my family, numbers that'd I'd been calling for years. I kept dialing and strangers kept answering, telling me that I'd made a mistake. And that is what I was hoping for, the mistake of all mistakes, the momentary death of my mother, and then her resurrection, like a hummingbird's heart warmed and beating once more.

Turning, I saw my daughters at my bedroom door, hanging on to hands, teary-eyed and frowning. They still appeared as fairies at the edge of a bleak garden, their faces so sweetly sad regarding what Georgia would later call my orphaning.

I waved them to me and then wrapped my arms around them the same way Mom used to wrap her arms around Aubrey and me when we were troubled. We fell together on the bed, sobbing. We had been painted black. Not on the outside, but on the inside, as quickly as a flock of butterflies appearing. *We had been painted black by his hands of death on one whom we loved.*

On the first day that I entered the sail loft, it had been almost a year since Mom's death, a year in which I had worked very hard to run from the truth of it. I stepped close to the Indian maiden bust on the mantel and studied the missing portion of her neck. It was as if her voice box had been slashed away. I rubbed my fingers along the soft and peaty trough. It was easy to imagine her floating on the water, her face toward the sky with her chin held high, as Mom's might be now, resting on a cloud of feathers. I wondered if the bust had been struck with something hard, or if like Mom, she had suffered one stroke, and then another?

On the sixth day of June, the first anniversary of Mom's death, I lifted the bust off the mantel, finding her heavier on her wooden base than I had expected, and discovering the side of her face that had been tucked to the brick wall damaged beyond repair, no doubt the last and final stroke.

What pain had Mom suffered when she died? None of us had dared to ask. The assisted-living nurse said that Mom simply threw her Ship of Dreams quilt back and then called to my older sister, Evangeline, *I'm ready.*

Evangeline, who had been there only minutes earlier, tucking Mom in for her afternoon nap after her visit with George—and the salmon jumped like rabbits and the blackflies were as thick as storm clouds—Evangeline, never imagining an afternoon dream might carry our mother away. Had she known, she would have stayed and called, *Mom, Mom.* Instead, she returned to find our mother neatly covered, her petite face and chin lifted toward the heavens, her eyes closed as if sleeping.

"I'm sorry," the nurse whispered, "but your mother got away."

Got away.

Evangeline told me months later that she laid her head on Mom's chest, listening for the *chug, chug, chug.* She prayed for a heartbeat, but our mother's heart had been plucked like a shiny object from a costume. Somewhere, a mighty crow flew with it.

Afterward, she bathed Mom's waning body, the soft milky-mother-body she would neither see nor touch again. While lifting to wash beneath Mom's arm, a last gasp of trapped air escaped, and hope lit through Evangeline's tears like a pin pushing through a veil. She said for the shortest second she hoped that she might be witnessing our mother's resurrection.

For reasons I don't yet understand, whenever I think of them together in these moments, I am reminded of an old photo. Mom is young and dressed in a dark skirt and ruffly blue blouse holding baby Evangeline, who appears big and heavy, but Mom is smiling so proudly that it seems as if her weight is no more than that of a beloved doll's.

After Mom died, Evangeline called George to return. There, they sat with Mom until the undertaker, who had grown up with both of them, drove along the Saint John River, arriving in the black hearse that had received many of our loved ones, the same black hearse that had carried our father away. There is no sadder time than when a loved one is carried away in a hearse. It is as if they have been stolen by a dark and mighty force. *Hearse.* It is a slender, forceful word. One that can puncture like a hunter's knife. Yet there is no synonym for it. *Hearse.* One simply finds it listed in the dictionary, immediately preceding the word *heart.*

To my brother and sister's surprise, the undertaker, Wendell, arrived with his mother accompanying him. When the hearse pulled into the driveway, Dot's white hair gleamed from the passenger's side. She and my mother had been friends for sixty years. I know that seeing Dot was a moment of joy for Evangeline and George. They did not see the hearse; they saw another loving mother coming to accompany their own.

Two days later, our hearts would follow that same hearse carrying Mom from the church to the cemetery in the valley where we grew up, along a narrow road through a woods, passing one deer and then another, standing still and blinking at the edge of the forest, some with lichen-covered antlers.

———

The maiden bust straight on was an elongated heart, her forehead much broader than her chin, her nose half-perky, half-long, her lips, half-thick, half-thin. Her eyes were closed and she was not as young face-on as she looked to be from the side. Her cheeks were sinking—this is where they say a woman loses her youth first—but she was amazingly peaceful-looking, her contentment present and overpowering her injuries. She seemed to be half-young, half-old, half-wonder, and suddenly her injuries simply faded.

I rubbed her throat, allowing myself to realize that the thing I missed most about my mother was her lilty, come-home voice. Then, I allowed myself to remember a mother with a wonderful mind, a talent for memorizing and metaphor, for writing and fable-telling and arranging beauty. Why had I not allowed myself to miss her until now? Because I was afraid of spiraling down. We all were.

When our father was driven away in the hearse, Mom was there to console us, humming and caressing us back from the freeze of his death, but now both of their chairs around our family table were empty, our mourning as deep as a hibernating sleep, our interiors slowed by its sludge, the synonyms of sorrow skillfully lassoing our vital organs and changing their names to distress, misery, and woe.

While cradling the bust, something from my last conversation with Mom returned. On the telephone, her mind had been clear and her voice as gentle as ever, unrushed. I had spent the evening doing laundry, and when I mentioned it, she said, *You write too well to be doing housework.*

My heart lifted. Mom did not often speak of my writing. When I began to write in my late twenties, she had encouraged me to paint instead, a curious thing, since I had no particular talent for painting. She had even arranged for me to work with her oldest brother, a respected painter. She said he would instruct me in the basics and I indulged her, but our meeting was mannerly at best. Uncle Rand had had his cancerous larynx removed, and every word he spoke was a struggle: gulpy, echoey, and strangely mechanical-sounding as it fought to exit the surgeon's makeshift hole in his throat. The hole was the only thing about him that did not bespeak elegance. Even though he kept it covered with a silk kerchief, it was easy to picture the crude wet opening, for as a child, I had once asked to see it.

During the lesson in his attic studio, my eyes kept wandering to his bookshelf. The complete works of C. S. Lewis, a series of biblical reference books, Malcolm Muggeridge. There was even one that had been written about my uncle: *R. H. Nicholson: Painter and Man of God*, and a book titled *Memoirs of a White Crow Indian*.

When I reached to touch the word *Indian* on the book's binding, my heart beat faster. Maybe I was an Indian. If so, who could blame Mom for wanting me to paint rather than write? Who knew what I might discover? But then, on the very night before she would leave this world, she was telling me to write, giving me permission to let go of domesticity, the thing that she had embraced so beautifully: her open arms and flowery smell, her masterful cooking and freshly ironed bedsheets, her flower arrangements already intuitively placed before the visitor's call.

She had instructed me to write as if she were softly singing. In retrospect, her instruction also sounded as if she were standing on a great precipice and calling back to me, as if she were already leaving. It reminded me of a painting of an Indian maiden that hung in my uncle's upstairs hallway, which he had painted. Often Mom and I stood admiring the naked maiden, standing at the edge of a high cliff over a waterfall. Beneath the maiden, a green pool shimmered and the full moon lit the mossy green of the cliff and made her skin shimmer, too. Everything was a gleaming shade of green, the girl and the water and the forest, as iridescent as a mermaid's fin. Whenever we took the noontime train to visit my uncle, Mom led me upstairs to see the painting.

Then I thought she probably loved the painting because she loved to swim. She had taught all of her children to swim, instructing us in the techniques of a strong stroke, and showing us how to roll our hips through the water, to use the water's momentum so our own energy might be saved. She taught us how to take in air and then expel it through a series of small bubbles, allowing us to remain underwater that much longer. And finally, she showed us how to move toward the air if we were ever trapped beneath an upturned canoe, or, God forbid, trapped in a sinking car.

Often I longed to have our favorite swimming hole to myself, to listen to the birds that gathered there—the whip-poor-wills and cowbirds, the mockingbirds and wrens—to swim beneath their songs. But even with Mom's good instruction, she never allowed her children to go swimming alone. Once on a particularly hot day when she was getting ready for summer guests, I begged to go for a swim. I was eight.

"Absolutely not," Mom said. She was pressing linen napkins and locked in a dreary stare, the iron's steam hissing up under her chin.

"Why not?" I fussed. "I'm a good swimmer."

Mom looked at me. There was a weight in her eyes as dark as the stones at the bottom of the creek. "Long before a child is born," she said, "a mother fears losing them. Let's not take any unnecessary chances."

Unnecessary chances. I saw the words. They paddled frantically between us in the iron's steam like children caught in an undertow.

Maybe Mom loved the waterfall painting because the maiden seemed to be about eighteen—her admitted forever age—or maybe she loved it because the girl looked so free, not seeming to care if people even knew she existed. At any rate, she always leaned into the painting with such wonder—her blue eyes crinkled and concentrating—that I could barely look away from the shimmering reflected in her face. It was the same way she sometimes looked at me.

Remembering the waterfall painting while we talked that last time made me miss her shimmering face and the softness of her hand as she took hold of mine, leading me up my uncle's narrow stairway, her smell as fresh as spritzed linens. How could I forget the iridescence washing over her, the look of anticipation on her face? It sometimes seemed as if she were about to dive into the pool of green herself. *Isn't this the most beautiful painting?* Once she removed it from the wall. On the back, someone had written, *For Deborah.* At the time, I did not think much of it, because I knew all the paintings in my uncle's home were tagged for loved ones, just as all the paintings in my own home were. But now I cannot help but wonder if there was a deeper message. *Why* was this painting for me? Was I an Indian maiden?

That last night, while Mom breathed words that brought back memories of an Indian maiden, I had no idea that she was about to dive and disappear, no idea that she was indeed standing on a great precipice. Was her melodious flight-light voice releasing me, telling me to write? Did she know that she was leaving and that I would lay my head on her chest no more—as I had done a few weeks earlier on her eighty-third birthday—listening to her beating heart as if listening for a promise of her longevity? *Chug, chug, chug.* Might you stay forever?

After, she held my face in her hands. Her eyesight was poor from macular degeneration, and I thought she was trying to get a good look at me. She smelled of lilacs and she smiled a shimmering smile of recognition, the same smile she had for the painting. At the time, I thought it was the smile of loving me, but maybe it was the smile of leaving me. Did she know that the two of us would never stand in front of that waterfall painting again? Did she know that the deer were preparing to view her as she passed to the valley, their wet eyes blinking? Had she sensed the letting-go of life? If so, she must have known that in the end, my writing would be the dive I'd need to take to find my way without her. Back to her. Back to myself. She must have known *that remembering the lovely things we have forgotten is one of the reasons for all art.*

On Mom's last birthday evening in May, my daughters had waltzed together in the main room at the assisted-living center. There was a visiting pianist playing Chopin. Mom watched her granddaughters dance while smiling and clapping to the waltz. After the pianist had packed up her sheet music and left, Mom told the girls to go and look out the window facing the street. When they had, she asked, "Can you see my home on the hill?" Her question was out of context, as some things sometimes were, and Georgia, sensing a stroke-induced skipping in her grandmother's memory, said, "Oh yes, Nannie. I see the lights. I do. Someone is waiting for you on the hill."

Where was my intuition then?

———

Next to the mantel and the woodstove are two six-over-six windows offering a bird's-eye view of the town dock. Beneath those windows is a battered trunk with several duck decoys and an old stereo. In front of the trunk are two wicker chairs, exact replicas of the chairs that were in our summer room at home, chairs that Mom and I often lounged in while reading or chatting with one another. It was there she often received my numerous tales of woes and confessions. It was there she instructed me in life.

I sit and swing my legs over the arms of one wicker chair while the other remains empty, holding the bust to my chest. A white butterfly flutters through the open door and skims over the cushions of the empty chair, the tips of its wings shimmering like a green pool of water beneath a waterfall.

These are some of the things that I found when I entered the sail loft twelve days ago, and these are some of the things besides a broken motherless heart that I brought with me: Mom's diaries and journals, a photo album of my family and ancestors, several novels, several empty notebooks, pencils and pens, candles, King Cole Tea from Canada, a navy-blue-and-white bathing suit, cutoffs, a worn white oxford shirt of my husband's, flip-flops, two orange-striped beach towels, sunglasses, sunscreen, a camera, a yellow bucket, and a painting of a sail loft done by my uncle, R. H. Nicholson. Although I don't believe he ever visited Castine, it hauntingly resembles the sail loft.

I also brought a lift-top desk from the home that my mother went to after she was orphaned at two, the home on the hill. I brought a cookbook called *Lost Recipes*, the *Eldridge Tide and Pilot Book*, and three framed photos that my brother George took of the backshore beach at sunset shortly after Mom died; the earth is dark, but the sky is bright orange, like the dot beneath a mother seagull's beak.

I brought an armload of freshly picked lilacs. And although I didn't know this on the first day that I entered the sail loft, I had come to find my way back to so many of the lovely and not so lovely things that I had tried to forget. To remember. Not merely because the present contained the past, but because my moral world depended on it. I needed to glue back the picture of my life. What were my two selves, my two sorrows? My loves and losses? And why had I been willing to take an unnecessary chance?

Part Two

one

$\mathcal{A}$s a girl, I used to steal a neighbor's pony, black and shaggy and sometimes lazy. I don't believe he had a name. I'd watched for years as he stood on a knoll in an open field, staked and chained, across the road from our home. The only time I saw his owner, Mr. Harris, was when he brought the pails of water and feed out to the field. Never once did I see him pat the pony before turning and going back to his little house under the hill. Sometimes if the patch where the pony stood had been eaten and worn bare, Mr. Harris moved his stake.

Mom said Mr. Harris was a man who had suffered a loss. And indeed, he walked with his shoulders caved around his chest, as if his heart had been plucked away. When I pressed her for details, she said that Mr. Harris's wife left him long ago, and the pony had belonged to her.

Through all seasons, the pony stood in that field. Like the Baptist church down the road or the tarry-smelling black bridge that stood above the creek near the crossroads, he became one of my constant touchstones. He was there when the strawberries arrived, the blueberries and blackberries, the cranberries and chokecherries. When it rained, his black coat glistened. When it was dry and hot, he rolled in the dust, and then stood looking ghostly. When the fall winds blew, his thickening coat quivered and his mane pointed sideways as if it were a weathervane. One winter day, after a snowstorm had turned icy, he glistened like a white sculpture. Later, the sun broke through, making him shimmer. The sight of him held Mom's attention just as it did mine, prompting her to tell me the story of the magnificent winged horse, Pegasus, born of the shed blood of Medusa.

When I was nine, I unhitched the pony's chain and climbed on him bareback for the first time. His coat was warm from baking in the sun and his strength was instantly transmitted into my legs, up through my very center, making me sit tall and proud. I remember that moment now as Pony receiving me. From that day on, I made a habit of him. With much prompting and a fair bit of kicking, he would saunter through the field. Once in a while, he took off with such speed that my hands turned blue hanging onto his withers. He could be so commanding that I thought of him as a super pony. Surely, he was a descendant of Pegasus, born of shed blood. In bed at night, my legs and bottom muscles ached and my palms smelled of his earthy dusty coat. Sometimes I licked my grimy hands and a wiry hair from his withers rolled onto my tongue. This, I slipped inside my pillowcase with the others.

One day I took him to the creek down in the field behind our house. Upstream was the deep and wide swimming hole where Mom often took us but never allowed us to go alone. Her fear of someone drowning was constantly reinforced by our father, who had been held underwater by a bully when he was three, and consequently never learned to swim.

It was an unusually humid summer day. All men and beasts seemed limp, wrapped in a steamy heat that the weatherman said was like a soggy woolen blanket over the entire province of New Brunswick. Even Mom was taking a break from the household chores, fanning her face with a folded newspaper on the verandah, her dreamy eyes barely registering me as I led Pony past. Probably too weary to surmise that I was taking him to the swimming hole, she simply smiled as if we were, Pony and I, a cool breeze lighting on her face.

Halfway down the path, I climbed down and led him along the line of raspberry bushes and alders and maple trees, along the flat hayfield that had been cut the week before, its sweet seedy smell wafting in the heat. The sheared hay was like sharp sticks pricking my bare feet. I twisted and jerked, ooh, ha, ooh. Finally, Pony stopped and blinked his dewy brown eyes. A glistening green moose fly buzzed at his head.

"What is it?" I asked, a shiver traveling up my neck, the same feeling I had when once finding broken eggs within a nest, and the gray liquid birds spilling from them. I thought perhaps Pony was afraid because we were heading into new territory, or maybe he was thirsty. I'd noticed that when I unchained him earlier his water pail had tipped over and was empty. A crow flew over and cawed twice, so screechy that it sounded like a warning. Somewhere in the distance, a mockingbird copied it, *Caaawww, caaawww.*

I touched his silken head.

Pony twisted his neck and nodded his head, his nose pointing behind us. Maybe he was trying to warn me of something, a bear hidden in the raspberry bushes or Aubrey following us, so he could tattle. Slowly he pushed with his flank, spinning me in a small circle, and nudging me with his head. I giggled, yet he continued, moving faster and faster until I surrendered, climbing onto his smooth warm back, then onward we went, my feet free of being pricked and scratched.

Reaching the creek, Pony turned without any prompting and walked north toward the deep swimming hole. Maybe before she departed, Mrs. Harris had brought him here to drink, or maybe he had seen it in a dream, dreamed the very day about to happen, and was now simply stepping into it.

At the swimming hole, he waded in until my feet were soaking in the tepid water. The creek was not running as it sometimes did, but was still from the dry days and nights. Except for the song of an occasional bird or the distant trickle of the small waterfall upstream, it was as quiet as any place one might see in a dream. A huge maple tree that grew on the opposite side of the water shaded us with the shimmering leaves that made a hushing chorus. In the tree, a cowbird began to call its gurgly notes, *bub-klo*, followed by a higher-pitched squeak, *seek-ki-seek, bub-klo-seek-ko-sek.*

I knew the brown-headed cowbird laid its eggs in the nests of other birds, and it made me smile as I sat comfortably in the nest of someone else's pony. The heck with Mrs. Harris, I thought, trying to spot the cowbird. You are mine now, Pony.

When Mom brought us swimming, we all jumped from the maple's low-lying limbs into the deep pool. Climbing into the tree for our first jump, a multitude of birds always flocked from its branches so powerfully that I imagined myself caught in their updraft. I imagined myself as one of them, *Seek-ki-seek.*

"Pony," I said, "the bloodsuckers are here. Wade deeper."

Mom always warned us not to linger in the shallows where bloodsuckers lay disguised on dark rocks in the warmer waters. She carried a saltshaker in her wicker basket in case one decided to attach itself. My brothers intentionally incited them. How they loved to shake the salt and watch the brown bloodsuckers shrivel and then drop away from their hands or the soles of their feet. Once, my cousin had unknowingly gone home with one in her bathing suit. When she undressed, she found it swollen to the size of a plum and sucking on her belly. Her mother extracted it right away, but she never went swimming again. To this day, I can see her standing at the water's edge, white socks and brown-laced shoes, fully clothed, while the other children splashed and swam about. Sometimes, I thought her a phantom. She often said that bloodsucker could have killed her—It could have sucked the life right out of me. I knew no different, listening to her tale of survival, and often watching her lifeless image at the shore, I thought perhaps it had.

I kicked Pony and he dipped his nose and slurped a drink, then clopped over the rocks until the creek water reached his flank, and then he swam in the swimming hole. I wrapped my arms around his neck and laid my head on his withers. They smelled of fresh earth plowed and baking in the sun, somehow equally of life and death the way I supposed a myth might. I thought of a hymn Mom often hummed while washing dishes, *In the sweet by and by, we shall meet on that beautiful shore . . .*

Of course, I knew Mom's story of a water horse that pulled the chariot of the sea god Poseidon, but I never dreamt that a pony could be a water horse. Why not? Hadn't all those times he'd taken off running, drumming across the wide field, spoken of his greater powers? Why hadn't I thought to bring him to the creek long ago?

Pony swam in a circle as if that were the water ring he once knew, even dipping until the two of us were completely submerged. I breathed by blowing out bubbles just the way I'd been taught. Maybe Mom knew that I'd someday swim with a magical horse. Maybe that was what she had prepared me for with all her tales and swimming lessons. What mother would not want it for her child?

The deep water was clear and a collection of large brown rocks made up its bottom. I had skinned my knees on those rocks countless times while diving, always imagining them as the bones of the earth, but who knew—maybe they were people turned to stone by Medusa. Anything seemed possible that day. I thought an unusually large rainbow trout shimmered by, but easily could have imagined it.

When we came to the water's surface, the sun was directly over the big maple tree. Its bright light dappled through the leaves and made diamonds on the water. I stretched out my fingers and touched them as we swam. Dad often said when we took walks or finished a glorious Sunday dinner that life didn't get any better. I felt that with Pony.

I recently read that swimming with horses is something offered at spas and exclusive resorts, marketed as a way to find one's eternal now, but until that day it was an activity only alive in one of Mom's recited myths, an activity I thought too beautiful to be real.

Pony finally tired and carried me to the shore. He shook his coat and I shook with him and then we traveled down along the stream, the creek water evaporating from us, slipping away like the feeling after waking from a beautiful dream. A cowbird followed along, eating the bugs that swirled around his swishing tail. We crossed the hot sheared hayfield cool and refreshed. Aubrey met us halfway up the path, licking a root beer Popsicle that dripped onto his hand, the clear brown color exactly like the water on the creek's bottom.

"Where have you been?" he asked.

It seemed an easy question, but I could not say for sure. Of course I knew the place and who had been there with me, but I did not know how to put it into words.

"To the swimming hole," I said, and left it at that.

"You're not supposed to go there alone."

"I didn't," I said. "I went with Pony."

Aubrey looked at me and then at Pony, as if he were weighing the possibility of an animal being a protective companion, and then he threw his

Popsicle stick and ran up the hill, fading like a mirage in the bright sun before he reached the verandah.

While I was chaining Pony to his stake, he licked my hand. His tongue was faded pink and as nubby as a raspberry, and it tickled. Again, I giggled. He padded his hooves and dust rose from the dry patch of earth, dusting our faces and powdering our lips. His mane shined. I combed it with my fingers, the creek's dampness still hidden at its roots. You deserve better. You deserve a real brush and a shady place to stand. If only this field had a tree.

Just then Aubrey hollered and waved from the road.

"*Rio Bravo* is coming on for the afternoon movie. Hurry. Stephen says we can watch with him."

Our brother Stephen was twelve, and although I could not have said this then, looking back, I know now that he'd already suffered the sorrow of a cruel teacher, and it sometimes left him irritable and moody. Yet, little did any of us know then that a second sorrow would come his way that fall, a shocking and painful stream of bullets on Halloween Eve, piercing stars of buckshot. And although he would survive the shooting, it would not only change him, but change us all.

Often, Stephen claimed the TV room as his own, sitting in Dad's La-Z-Boy and playing the arms of the recliner with his drumsticks, staring straight ahead at the soundless moving picture on the television. It was a small room with long pretty windows at each end. Mom had painted the walls pink and the corner shelves white. There she had arranged the antique collections, which she had started for each of us: small milk pitchers and Toby jugs, china dogs, miniature pharmacy bottles that she found along the old fence line, and later, there would be a row of tiny black ponies made by Royal Doulton.

We watched *Rio Bravo*, not fans of John Wayne, but of Dean Martin, because he reminded us of Dad, his dark shiny skin and black hair, his easy laugh and way, his relaxed wrist and limp fingers holding a cigarette.

I glanced at Stephen as he watched the movie, lanky in the La-Z-Boy, his dark blue eyes hooded with heavy brows and a strong forehead. His gray pageboy cap was resting on the back of his head and his curly black hair was damp around his ears. I somehow felt tethered to his mystery sorrow that day. It was as if an invisible string was stretched taut and pulling between us. He glanced at me, but said nothing. Searching his eyes, I felt a wilderness. After the shooting that fall, the wilderness would stretch and become so vast between us that at times, I thought our taut tethered string would break.

The next day I couldn't wait to get to Pony. Even the *Rio Bravo* horses could not compare. All night on my pillow full of withers, I'd dreamt of swimming with him, dreaming of my eternal now. Already the morning sun burned in the sky like a blister. I ran as fast as I could up through the field to find Pony on his side, covered in dust. From a distance, I thought he was only resting from a roll, but up close he was quiet and still. His open eye stared up. There was nothing soft-looking about his eye anymore. It appeared stony, a wet Medusa rock beneath the creek. Had she come in the night and stared him down? I turned to run for Mom, tripping over the tipped water pail, and then crawled back to him and tried to roll him up, pushing and pushing. "Keep rolling," I cried. "Please."

He was a wall of pony, beyond dead weight. Much later in life, I will recall those moments as a battle with death. I tried to open Pony's mouth so I could spit into it, but his teeth were locked together and the parting of his lips offered nothing but a sinister stare. His breath smelled of shriveled apples. I pulled so hard on his tail that great clumps of it came out into my hand and then laid around us like collapsed and mourning kittens.

Finally, I climbed and lay on the flank that had made me surrender the day before, the warm flank that had rescued me so my hay-pricked feet would stop hurting. As I ran my fingers through his dusty mane, no mythical power came from his body. Even the roots of his mane were dry and dusty.

I slid off to listen for his heartbeat, but it seemed no heart had ever been there. Where was it? I rubbed him frantically all over, up and down, hoping my hands that felt like they were burning, my first flamed hands of loss, might revive him.

When I touched the swollen bloodsucker on his side—bloated translucently red and pulsing like a heart itself—I thought my burning hand would explode. Immediately, I tried to pull and then pry its inflated body off, but it clung as if part of Pony now, that horrible thing that I thought then must have killed him, the same way one had almost killed my cousin. Looking back, though, I will come to picture it as Pony's pulsing heart, still beating, rising out of him, the thing that he'd left behind to show he was once alive. We'd swum in a pool of diamonds. Yes. Is it not the beating heart of a loved one we try so hard to hear after they are said to be dead?

Years later, Mom said she heard me calling that day. At first, she thought a bird was being attacked, the way I cawed such loneliness. *Your outcry*, she called it. I do not remember.

Nor do I remember her rushing up the hill and pulling me away from Pony, nor do I remember Mr. Harris coming up over the hill. I do not remember the mockingbird that sat on the telephone wire, imitating me as I passed beneath it while hanging on to my mother's hand, *Caaaawwww. Caaaawwww.*

I do not remember Aubrey sitting on the verandah step, patting our white-and-yellow-spotted Sailor, and bursting into tears when he saw me, nor do I remember Stephen's anxious hooded teary eyes as I passed him in the doorway. This is the closeness of siblings, the invisible tugging string that knots their sorrows together. It was one of the few times that I saw Stephen cry. Yet years later, when he told me in detail about the night that he was shot, his eyes pooled once again. He said getting shot was exactly like they portrayed it in the Westerns. Your body goes one way and your cap another. And after, you're so thirsty that you think you will die. The image of his bleeding body, his salted thirst, his pink boy tongue, will lift the stretching wilderness between us and bind us forever in a knot.

I do not remember Dad coming home early to comfort me, nor do I remember the backhoe that lifted Pony onto a truck bed, and then hauled him to the dump. I do not remember much about staying inside the house for the rest of that summer. I know I ripped up a pencil drawing of my profile that

Uncle Rand had sketched while visiting us. Its pieces still lay hidden in the pages of my childhood Bible. I know I tried to read, but couldn't. Even one of Mom's recited myths could not hold my attention. I know Stephen was good to me, and Aubrey never far from my side. Sometimes Mom begged me to go swimming with her, to cool off, but I wouldn't. Instead I pictured myself standing as a phantom at that water's edge.

I do remember Dad cradling me in his La-Z-Boy, letting me rest my head on his chest and rubbing my ear while he watched the news or *Front Page Challenge*, and I remember Mom often brushing and braiding my hair while I sat at the window, keeping a watch over the empty field. Their sorrow was so palpable to me that sometimes I checked my own pulse. Still I could not pull myself away from the day that I found Pony dead. Deep down, I wondered if I was being punished for stealing him.

Years later, waking in the night, I had a vision of a young girl running toward me from a great distance. Her long black hair was braided and her green eyes sparkled and when she stopped breathy in front of me, wearing a sleeveless white eyelet blouse and a calico skirt, I realized that I was looking at myself from long ago. Slowly my lips turned downward and my face began to fade as if I were seeing myself the way Pony saw me as I raced toward him that day, watching me with his one stony eye as he slipped away as if to say, What is your name? I can't remember your name.

———

In the fall, with Mr. Harris's permission, Dad planted a sugar maple on the patch where Pony had died, watering it every day until the earth froze. This is how Dad often healed himself, beneath a tree, and it is what he knew to do for me. He had no way of knowing how Pony had swum in the creek under the great maple with me on his back, no way of knowing how the leafy tree had shaded us and showered us with diamonds made of sunlight, for I hadn't told a soul. Watching Dad plant the tree, I complained of its scrawniness.

"Like ponies," he said, "trees do not have to be big to attract attention."

This was Dad's regard for trees, for the maple and the oak, the fir and the pine, the elm and the aspen. And this was his regard for my loss. When he finished planting the tree, he took my hand and we walked toward home, he pacing out our walk with the planting shovel. Tall and dark and limber.

"I almost lost a friend once," he said.

"Almost only counts in the game of horseshoes," I said, but he continued with the story anyway. It was a story of Amos, his friend whom he'd recently visited on the reservation. Little did I know waiting in the car that I was watching a man who had once been tied up in his canoe by two drunken men. After, the men flipped the canoe upside down and pushed it into the river. Dad said that Amos was eventually rescued by someone who had spotted the canoe floating downriver.

"He could have disappeared forever," Dad said. "I often think of that. Especially when I haven't seen him in a while."

I did not hear the whole story of Amos's mishap until after my father's death. On a February night, while taking an evening break from the funeral home, where the aroma of too many roses was stifling and beginning to smell exactly to me like the letting go of life, Amos appeared beyond the parking lot, in the shadows of a stark tree with limbs reaching up to the cold moonlit sky. He was smoking with his wide chiseled face and crooked nose present only in its silhouetted shape, like the face of a great cliff. A man so tall and sturdy that it was hard to picture him bound in a canoe. Your father saved me once, he said, passing his cigarette, just as he had passed it to Dad many times.

I took a long drag and then blew it out. Really, Amos. How is that?

He pulled me from the river. I'd been tied up in a canoe by two men.

But Dad didn't know how to swim, I said, passing the cigarette back. He was afraid of the water.

Amos flicked the cigarette and its orange glow arched in a semicircle before landing somewhere in the crowded parking lot. He stepped forward, resting both hands on the top of my head as if to bestow a blessing. He swam that day.

Then he continued with his tear-filled testimony. The weight of his hands and the image of my father swimming deafened me in the most beautiful way. For a moment, I swam on Dad's strong back beneath the water, just as I had swum on Pony's. Amos's firm hands felt baptismal and I began to cry, not for the father I knew, but for the one that had moved beyond us to become a myth. The father of wonder. The one that I would never see on this Earth again, but who would sometimes appear in the guise of spirit men like Amos, some along forest trails and once, beneath a reaching tree.

A few months after Dad's death, I stood at the edge of the road by our home, admiring the tall maple tree he had planted so long ago. It was spring and near sundown and water trickled along a trail in the ditch. I had left Mom in the house drying the supper dishes and humming *In the sweet by and by, we shall meet on that beautiful shore, In the sweet by and by . . .*

Slowly, the thin shape of Dad appeared beneath the tree, leaning on a shovel. It was not my loving father that I contemplated then, but the shovel with its many meanings. How a shovel could dig a hole for someone to be buried in and forever gone or a shovel could dig a hole where a seed could be planted. I knew then that the smell of fresh-dug earth was always the same, no matter its purpose. It smelled of being plowed, of being turned over. It smelled equally of life gone by and of life to come. It smelled of myth.

Walking home after Dad planted the tree, he had turned at the road, curling his tanned and handsome fingers around the shovel's wooden handle.

"Nice," he said, looking back. "I say we call it Pony-tree."

"Stupid," I said, and raced home ahead of him.

"It's how you choose to see it," he called after me.

Not the dead pony, but the tree. Not the missing father, but the earth that is always ready to be dug, turned, and touched, and the scent of it lingering on the hands of those who continue to plant the seeds.

Watching the bare branches of Pony-tree as the sun set, a shadow was cast that had my father's gangly shape. I thought of the universal agreement that the craft of reproducing human figures had begun by the outlining of a man's shadow. I read that the erudite Pliny the Elder wrote in the thirty-fifth book of *Natural History* that a potter's daughter sometime in the middle of the first century AD had fallen in love with a foreign youth, and when it was time for him to leave, she traced the outline of his shadow on a wall.

Standing there, I understood the girl's need to outline or draw what would soon be missing. I understood her desperation. I reached out and followed the shape of Dad's shadow, my finger swirling like an eddy in the creek.

two

My first spiritual conversion took place when I was five years old on a swing in my cousin's backyard. It was a bright summer day and we had just returned from Vacation Bible School at the Baptist church on the knoll. Red cherry Kool-Aid stained our lips. Kristy had given me an underdog and I had swung high enough to see the waving hayfield that surrounded my home across the road. At the highest point, just before the swing started backwards, my heart seemed to leap from my chest, hanging suspended in the air. Of course, I could not see it, only felt it playfully and momentarily absent, before I began my descent and we were reunited.

Kristy grabbed the swing's ropes, holding on until I swayed to a complete stop. Between the whines of a distant chain saw, a white-throated sparrow was singing in the petunia beds nearby, *Oh, sweet Canada*. I pictured its pure white throat and dark bill, its black-and-white-striped head with patches of yellow. Once I'd found a song sparrow nest near the creek. It was in the root of an old maple tree, cleverly disguised with pine needles and wood chips, but not cleverly enough. Something had broken all of the tiny blue and speckled eggs except for one that was a different color. A gray slime had dried on the broken shells. I knew the mother bird would not return now that the nest had been disturbed, so I lifted the untouched egg with reddish-brown specks and let it rest in my palm. It was a brown-headed cowbird egg and as weightless as a blown kiss.

I carried the egg home and kept it in a tiny dish on my dresser, hoping a chick would someday appear, even though Mom said the chick would simply evaporate without the love of its mother. When my cousins or friends visited, it was the thing they went to first. Some hovered over the brown-speckled shell and some rolled it delicately about in the dish, but to my surprise, no one ever broke the cowbird egg. It was as if they knew the promise of life had been held within the shell, and like the empty tomb of Christ, it still somehow held a promise. To this day, it is wrapped in a Kleenex and sealed in a jelly jar, stashed in the red wooden trunk that holds my childhood belongings. Once I dreamed of the song sparrow shells fully restored and gathered on my dresser with the cowbird egg.

That day, Kristy stood in front of me, clinging tightly to the ropes of the swing, her cherry breath sweet on my face. Her eyes were blue and freckled like the cracked sparrow eggs, her thick strawberry-blonde hair cropped short. She was so opposite of me that I was in love with everything about her. I loved her house, which was newer and I thought nicer than our rambling homestead that had once belonged to my grandparents. I loved Kristy's mother Ruth, who sat in a kitchen rocking chair in the evenings after all her household duties were finished, smoking while reading a novel, and scolding anyone who interrupted her. I loved that there was always a frosted cake under a glass dome on their kitchen counter, my favorite being a chocolate one that Aunt Ruth made with Miracle Whip. It was a river of silk in my mouth. I loved Kristy's little sisters, Nancy and Lisa, and her big sisters and big brothers, eleven in all. I was from a family of only seven children, and so in another way, Kristy had more. Yet we were indefinably united, all from the same great Corey clan whose brother-fathers were our living myths, so strong and indestructible-appearing that it never occurred to us that they would someday give way to age and disease. When my father was dying, he told my sister that he never once thought of being old. *I was too busy ramming through the woods.*

Kristy's father, Uncle Fraser, was a man who constantly grinned and lit-erally talked out of the side of his mouth, patting children's heads when they passed. He was a man with stories he could barely contain, his body round, his face round and red as if it might explode from them, though some of the redness was no doubt from the drinking benders he sometimes took, for the Corey men played as hard as they worked, and once in a great while, even cried as hard as they laughed.

I loved the huge weeping willows in Kristy's yard, trees that she would eventually be married beneath. I loved the cascading flower boxes on the sunporch windows and the erupting vegetable gardens beyond the large lawn, and the little outbuildings, one a playhouse with old furniture, big-people furniture where the children of the neighborhood relived their families' lives: dying grandmothers, storytelling dads, a smoking mother, a religious mother, mean brothers, weeping sisters, new babies being born, doctor visits, stillborn lambs, election suppers, bridal showers, shotgun weddings, shivarees, tent meetings, baptisms, hymn sings, and quiet, absolute quiet. Stillness. Sometimes we just sat back on the old sofa in the playhouse and looked up at the rafters, lulled by the songbirds singing, and tucked by the hills like a collection of eggs in a nest in the root of tree. The playhouse had once been a chicken coop, and on occasion, a tiny white feather floated down from its rafters. Watching its descent, we thought we were receiving a message from God.

I loved Kristy even though she sometimes made fun of me for not speaking clearly. Lying in the ditch by my mailbox, I often called to her—Kitty, can you come or'wer—only to have her put her hands on her hips and say, "Geez, Debbie, when are you going to stop talking like a baby?"

I didn't understand the way she cast me off for my crooked words. My parents had waited patiently for me to say something decipherable and were thrilled when I finally did. But that day on the swing, the day that Kristy pulled the ropes to a halt, she studied my face as if I were the most important thing in the world to her, as if I were the promise of resurrection held in an empty tomb.

"Do you want to get saved?" she asked.

I gnawed at my bottom lip, picturing the men and women who fell on the church altar at the Sunday-night services. Some were poor, and one bedraggled young woman named Missy went every time there was an invitation. Each time, sobbing as if the wooden altar she sprawled on was a body that she'd always been searching for. After, standing and grinning, her eyes would be glassy like those of a child who had glimpsed a wild thing sleeping beneath a bush. They held excitement, but also a tinge of fear.

"Yes," I said. "I do want to get saved."

If Kristy had it or was peddling it, I wanted it. Just as I wanted her huge house and yard, her sparrow-laden petunia garden, her short shorts and belly shirts and her boy haircut, her playhouse with the old unplugged fridge, and her high-reaching swing that could pluck my heart away.

"Then bow your head," she said.

I did, staring down at her yellow flip-flops and hot-pink, sloppily painted toenails.

"Close your eyes," she ordered.

Kristy prayed a short quick prayer for Jesus to wipe my soul clean. I pictured his hand like my teacher's hand, wiping chalk from the blackboard, all my sins wiped away as quickly as a lesson learned.

I opened my eyes and Kristy's eyes were as blue as the sky beyond, checking mine.

"Good," she said, as if something in my eyes revealed my newfound salvation, as if she saw the wild beast sleeping there.

I sat as still on the swing as before Kristy started praying, but something inside had been lifted, not the way my heart lifted away while swinging, but now it felt secure yet also suspended, like a helium balloon that had floated to the ceiling and would always stay there, plump as a plum, its string securely in my Savior's hand.

My elation propelled me off the swing and I ran as fast as I could toward home, hollering for Mom long before I'd crossed the road without looking, my hovering heart steadying me like a parachute.

"Mom," I called, throwing back the screen door, which whined open and then quickly whined closed, snapping like the cover of a tightly hinged box. "Mom, Kitty saved me."

Mom was at the stove preparing lunch and her face was without expression, as if wiped clean of all thoughts and feelings, as if she were simply a blank blackboard. Touching her stirring hand that held the wooden spoon and breathing short breathy breaths, I said, "I'm, ha, a, ha, a Christian, ha, now, eh-ha, eh-ha, eh-ha."

Running home, I had run the play of the Rapture over in my head, with me as one of its many stars. I'd heard that a person's life passed before them when they died, so I figured maybe my future could pass before me when I was born again. Maybe one of the star Rapture roles had been waiting just for me.

I cannot remember what Mom was making for lunch. I wish I could. Perhaps it would signify something and let me build an understanding from metaphor—my own seven loaves and fishes, my water to wine—but I only remember the swirling navy pattern of her dress, which was like a raging sea, and her white starched apron strings pulled tightly at her curving waist.

"Kitty saved me," I said again, searching Mom's eyes that seemed held in another time.

"Kristy can't save you," she finally said, still staring. "Jesus has to."

Her words were soft-sounding, but they crashed over me like thundering waves. Within them, my breath was sucked away and my buoyant heart went with it, washed away, just as my sins had been a few minutes earlier. Then, I could not feel my heart's whereabouts. My chest felt vacant and my face felt as if it had fallen vacant, too. The blank face of an Amish doll. My features had evaporated like an unborn chick. And then my face became hard, feeling fragile, like it might break as easily as an eggshell from the weight of the mother bird.

Looking back, this is my first memory of feeling featureless, and one of my strongest memories of my heart as a palpable thing, subject to atmospheric change. The cleansing winds of salvation had made it bellow and float while my mother's proclamation had punctured it beyond its bellowing abilities. Her proclamation dripped over me, dank and chilling, causing my first migraine headache, one of many that will find me again and again in the years to come. That was the moment my heart insisted that I acknowledge the capsizing capabilities of its potential weight. It was not a balloon to play with. It was something to be managed and guarded. If not, I might give it to the wrong person and then be destined to damnation.

I went out to the verandah and sat down on the white bench. Dad would be coming home for lunch soon, his shiny car rising over the knoll by the Baptist church and racing toward us. The sun was still shining, the sparrows still singing, but the heat was now oppressive. I knew that I had been saved on the swing, felt the rise of it. I didn't know who caused it, Kristy or Jesus, and I didn't want it to matter. I did not want my heart earthbound and mired, buried beneath the waves of my mother's judgment.

I touched my lips and they were sore as if someone had punched me in the mouth, or perhaps my witnessing words had pounded them on the way out. Words that lost their shape and now blew like smoke rings over the hayfield before me. Much later, I will recall it as a blurry hinterland. I watched the smoke rings go, considering them a precursor to something worse. To Hell. They came from the ashes of my first smoldering headache. Many years later, a doctor will tell me those recurring smoke rings were called auras.

Who knew how many loads of laundry Mom had done that morning, how many rooms had been tidied up and beds made. Who knew how many phone calls she had dealt with or prayer chains she had committed to, or how many of her children had already been comforted or encouraged or taught. Just the day before, she had spent a long time listening to me read from the front page of the *Daily Gleaner*, helping me with the words and encouraging me. We were sitting on the verandah and when I overcame a particularly hard word, enunciating it clearly, she patted my head as if I were a kitten.

Perhaps Mom was tired or perhaps she had been standing at the stove, questioning God's existence or longing for an old love, or maybe she feared a daughter's conversion, which she had not witnessed. Only later would I learn of her mother's tragic fall in a Pentecostal church.

When it came to the godly, Mom must have feared for my safety. She did not want me flying high on another's swing, in case I were to fall. Years later, she told me that my grandmother had been encouraged to speak in tongues and had been placed on a chair for the congregation to witness. She fell and hit her head on the altar, and later, she died.

After her funeral, my grandfather heard from a neighbor what had happened to his wife in that church. Immediately, he walked to the church and retrieved the ladder-back chair that she had been forced to stand on, hanging it in his bedroom on a hook, the way a Shaker would. He died not long after, his heart sagging sideways like a burst balloon. Like his wife, he was forty-nine years old.

Before Mom and her siblings were divided up and sent to live with family and friends, they burnt the ladder-back chair in the woodstove. Not for revenge, for they, like their parents, were pacifists, but because they had no father to gather wood and they were cold. Mom said to them it was an unfamiliar chair, unlike the ones around their kitchen table that represented family. Family.

Family, the word floating down from Mom's lips, like a feather from the playhouse rafters. Like a message from God.

At five years old, though, I did not know these stories, and Mom's reaction to my conversion left me confused. I thought she would be happy. I thought my being saved might have been one of the miracles that she was expecting as she often sped to church with me in the backseat, my palms out the window catching the wind. What lines of destiny did the breeze print on them? What did my future hold?

I thought Mom might congratulate me the way she did the other newly saved after the altar calls. Even bedraggled Missy's renewed proclamations and wild eyes warranted hugs. I thought Mom might predict what role I'd be given in the Rapture. Surely a mother who worshipped and prayed on her knees daily must have an inside track to God's plan. But instead, this day would not only be the beginning of my headaches, but of me attaching to my sleek father, to his playfulness and humor.

I would also turn inward. Even though I was starting to speak clearly, while practicing reading the newspaper, I would speak less. I would be careful of rushing forward with exciting news in case of a disappointing response, my words betraying me. I would live in fear of being erased, of my lips feeling bruised, of my forehead bursting with pain.

Instead, I would be still, lying in the hayfields and watching the changing skies, listening to the birds. I liken the hideous cawing crow to Mom's scolding of proper ways. I wandered at the edge of the field where the big old maple tree and raspberries grew, and an old wire fence collapsed and twisted among the alders. Sometimes, I ate the raspberries or scratched words on the maple trunk with a rusty nail, clustering them together as if they had been first shaken in my hands and then thrown against the tree like dice. Sometimes I closed my eyes and touched the words as if they were Braille. I licked them, nubby and indented on my tongue just like raspberries. Scratched out, they could not hurt me. They were like wild animals suddenly awake and tamed. They were my pets, a dancing menagerie, a traveling show of mean and vicious words. Crow in a mommy suit. Piss-ant. Ass. Stink-face.

A few days ago I saw a black Lab tied outside town hall. He had a tattered floppy doll in his jaws and was sitting up straight, holding it proudly, yet his leash was tied so tightly to the lamppost that he could barely move. He was not free to play with his prized possession, to shake his head and run and toss it in the air. I saw that doll as his salvation and the tight leash as the dog's religion, and I remembered Mom and loved her more than ever. If at the heart of truth is love, as some say, then what difference does it make how we discover it or feel it for the first time? What difference does it make how we run and toss it in the air or let it fill our hearts?

After running home that day, I wished for Mom to take me in her arms, into her clothing of wild sea. Then, I would have stayed at her side. I would have touched and noted the broken eggshells and then smelled the omelet cooking, watching the cheddar cheese melt as she slid the spatula around the edges, releasing it from the heat.

Surely, the story of her mother's death and the legalism of her chosen church must have sometimes confused her. Surely, it was difficult to abide by every rule. And what if she didn't? What would happen to her? To her children? Still, she often glowed with light. Maybe not on that day, but I can't dispute her lifelong example, her prayer knees broadened from years of wear, her orphan testimony, her love for family. Family.

For a time, I learned to be most comfortable beneath a tree. There, I created my own myths and monsters, scratching out the mean words that could have grown inside me, crowding my heart for good, turning it as hard as stone. Instead, I released them on the tree, and the tree absorbed them.

Recently, I read that if a person wants to redeem confusing times, they have to approach the world with charity. The key is charity. At the heart of truth is love, and if we attempt to explicate or witness truth without charity, we betray it.

This statement took me aback. The article advised that the way to lubricate a confusing encounter is not by backing away and turning it into some kind of private cultural myth, as I had done with Mom, but to come to it with charity, respect, and love.

For years in remembering that day, I remembered it without charity. I pictured it as an overexposed photo, something that had gone wrong, my words sucked away, but seeing the tied black dog began to change that. Instead I remembered how very disciplined Mom was, staying faithful within the perimeter of her faith and its rules and domesticity and marriage and family. Surely, she sometimes dreamed of being rescued, be it a redeemer or a renegade. Surely, there were days when she must have wanted to run.

Mom's reaction that day sent me on a journey of scratching words on trees. How I cursed the crow as I carved my first words into that tree. Today, I do not know the splatter of paint on canvas or the digging of clams or the hauling of boats; I do not know the business of healing or building or finance; I do not know what it is to wash the body of a dead loved one as my grandfather did, or as my sister did for our mother. I only know the scratching of words, and I wonder if the habit, which I started at the foot of that tree, was the beginning of my way to the sacred, cutting the dark rough bark with the rusty nail until the soft interior revealed itself, veined and living like the palm of a hand, waiting to be taken.

three

When I was eighteen, my mother admitted that at my age, she'd had two love choices—my father, and a pilot whom she had dated before he left for World War II. By the time the pilot returned from duty, Mom had married Dad and was expecting her first child. The pilot soon moved away, but not before telling Mom that he couldn't believe a good girl like her had married a man who drank and caroused.

Even before Mom admitted this, I knew of her old love, because she kept his letters in a velvet crimson hatbox on her top closet shelf. The letters were tied with a thin purple ribbon and pinkish dried mayflowers were knotted in the bow. As a child, I used to sneak the hatbox down from the shelf and then carefully remove the letters. The sky-blue handwriting on the envelopes—sixteen in all—was small and concentrated, and the envelopes smelled of cedar, just as Mom's closet did. Rubbing my fingers over my mother's name and address on the envelopes made me feel connected to her past. I pictured her as she appeared in older photographs, young and wearing a belted dress, her cropped brown hair glittering and her chin tucked as she smiled that thrilling broad smile.

Each letter was in a thin airmail envelope with the image of a small airplane zooming across the upper left corner. The writing paper inside appeared worn and wrinkly, and as translucent as Mom's porcelain skin. All of the letters began with *My Love*, and ended with *Yours, Del*.

Whenever I untied the ribbon, a few dried mayflowers crumbled and then landed on my lap like dust. I couldn't remember a spring going by that Mom didn't go into the damp forest near the creek to gather the mayflowers that grew amidst the moss, their light pink blossoms having the same cast as tears pooling in a young girl's eyes. Once she arrived home from the forest with a bouquet and news of a doe with antlers.

"Amazing," she kept saying, pacing about the kitchen, the flowers held in her hands like a wedding bouquet. "She was so lovely. Her antlers were like velvet. And she kept watching me as if there was something she wanted me to know. Honestly, it was amazing. Even a buck doesn't have his antlers this time of year. They've lost them by now."

"Are you sure it was a doe with antlers?"

"Yes," she said, smiling. "I'm sure. And it means something. It does."

"Why would a doe grow horns?" I asked.

"Necessity," she said matter-of-factly.

"What do you mean by necessity?"

Mom stopped pacing and faced me. I thought I saw a dewdrop shimmering on her cheek.

"Protection," she said firmly, as if it was common knowledge, as if everyone in the valley where we lived understood a horned doe's nature. I wondered then if the doe was born with horns or had perhaps grown them during some hardship, or if perhaps it was part of some miraculous transformation, a crowning of sorts, and I wanted to ask her but didn't.

The mayflowers that Mom gathered always sat for weeks in a large white milk pitcher on her maple dresser. Now, I'm not surprised that she kept the bouquets in her bedroom, admiring them, I suppose, as Dad slept next to her, or in the early mornings after Dad had left for work, or even gazing at them lit by the moonlight while he stayed out late carousing with his drinking buddies.

Thirteen years before Mom died, we were picking strawberries in a U-pick field near home. The June sun was warm and had turned her arms pink, and had also encouraged the berries to release their sweet watery perfume. Rows of glistening plants stretched over the undulating green hills. We were among a small group of pickers filling our berry boxes and chatting when someone called Mom's name, Georgia. We looked at each other, listening again for the voice that sounded both near and far away—Georgia.

Mom stood holding her overflowing box of berries while the shadow of a tall man came near and shaded her. Nearby, one of the pickers was humming *I come to the garden alone, while the dew is still on the roses.*

The shadow-man said Mom's name again, this time with relief, *Georgia*, as if he had been looking for her for a very long time. Mom tilted her berry box so quickly that I thought a shock must have gone through her, and for the shortest moment I worried that she might be having another stroke. Berries dropped and rolled, gathering around her new white sandals like plump drops of blood. Seconds later, her questioning gaze turned into an expectant smile, her chin held high, her cheeks blushing to match her sun-kissed arms.

Mom did not answer the man, but reached her hand out instead. Once they touched, she smiled and said, "Why, hello, Del."

"My," he said in a deep and powerful voice.

And the voice I hear, falling on my ear . . .

"It's been a long time," Mom said.

"Seems like yesterday." Del was in no hurry to let go of Mom's hand.

I pictured their palm prints pressed together like a sealed love letter. It appeared in that moment that each of their palms might hold matching aborted lifelines. The saccharine scent of the strawberries seemed to envelop them until they were so separated from me that I witnessed them as if I were watching a scene on a large screen, my mother's handsome wide cheeks and blazing blue eyes, and Del with his deep voice. They turned and walked away, between a plethora of heavy-laden plants. They were no longer touching, just side by side. *And he walks with me and he talks with me, and he tells me I am his own.*

Watching them, I was not a daughter anymore. A daughter would have been jealous on behalf of her adored father. In the same way that Mom's old love now walked by her side, I seemed to walk, too, as her shadow-woman, basking in the sheer and living sensuality that seemed to be pulsing through her. Nothing about it felt wrong. In fact, it somehow held the notion of restoration, as if the two of them had been broken apart and for a time turned to dust, but were now being condensed into a loving shape by the sun. As they moved farther away, they became brighter and more distinct and glistened as if dusted with sugar. Before they parted in the distance, they appeared as one, their bodies melding together, their heads tilting sideways creating the shape of a heart.

The day after Mom saw Del, she seemed to have a new lift in her step, as if shaking his hand had restored that aborted lifeline, making her young again. We talked about her old love, and her voice was lush, and also breathy, as if she had just sprinted through the strawberry field. I remember thinking, *She won't be able to sustain this, she won't.* Mom had just turned seventy and was accustomed to her heart walking rather than sprinting. She had recently been given stronger medication for recurring angina. As I watched her happily yet somehow frantically busying herself in the kitchen, it occurred to me that her good-girl beliefs were not protecting her from the temptation of Del. The thought was as startling as the sight of a mismatched egg in a bird's nest. Instantly, I knew that one of the misconceptions I had about Mom's faith was that its protective shell protected her from temptation—that because she believed, it was always easy to be good.

While we sat at the table stemming strawberries, I asked Mom how she was resolving her feelings for Del. She pursed her lips, which had a tinge of crimson like the hatbox that held her love letters.

"Well," she said, "an unresolved love from one's past isn't necessarily a bad thing."

"Why is that?" I asked.

She took a deep breath that sounded both determined and necessary.

"Whenever times are hard between your father and me, I can remind myself that someone else loves me." Her voice wavered.

I felt like her shadow-woman again, like a friend listening rather than a daughter, and I had the momentary feeling of graveness, as in, fraught with danger or harm. I noted, too, that Mom spoke of this past love in the present tense, *loves.* I wondered if that was what unresolved love was, something always present, and ready to bubble up through one's earth like a rushing spring, a guarantee of still-living waters. Yet, there was also a lack of conviction in her voice, as if she were simply thinking out loud, or perhaps trying to incorporate some trendy advice that she'd read in her *Ladies' Home Journal*. I knew she did not approve of infidelity, but she obviously knew what it felt like to want another. How could she not? All those nights waiting for my father alone in her bed, curled on her side while pink mayflower tears streamed onto her pillow.

———

Dad's occasional drinking jags could last a few days. When he came home, it was always under the cloak of darkness. Often we'd hear him singing "Tiny Bubbles" before the car's motor was even shut off.

One night, Aubrey and I spied on him from an upstairs window. Like Nabokov, we were "poor go-to-sleepers," and on that particular night we blamed the noisy spring peepers. To entertain ourselves we had been sitting on the floor at the double windows in the upstairs hallway, speculating on the alien that we'd read about in the *National Enquirer*. The alien had been found in a spaceship that had crashed in a field, and was now being hidden by the US government. We had conjured up several theories of what the alien might be like, and although we disagreed on size and intelligence, we did agree on the fishbowl head and slippery mushroom-like skin. We'd been surveying our dark yard and the hayfields beyond in hopes of one having crashed near us. Although neither of us had said it, I knew we both coveted the front page of the *Enquirer*. Many nights I fell asleep with the grainy image on that cover in my head, a short alien standing in a cage between Aubrey and me, his wrinkly long fingers wrapped around the bars like dead ivy, and his saucer-eyes pleading to be freed. BROTHER AND SISTER FIND ALIEN LURKING IN YARD.

When Dad arrived home late that night, we quickly shifted our attention. He began banging the driver's door with his shoulder and mumbling. Finally, he crawled through the open window, landing headfirst on the driveway, where he rolled quickly to his feet and then stood all in one action, as loose as a Slinky. *Jack be nimble, Jack be quick, Jack jump over the candlestick.*

Aubrey and I ducked our heads, giggling so loud that it woke our dozing mother, and then we all listened to Dad's awkward entrance into the kitchen, banging and cursing. When not drinking, he returned to us like a boomerang, snapping into the hand of our hearts, but when drunk, he could be cumbersome and hard to hang on to, like an alien with slippery skin.

Once inside, he might call for Mom from the bottom of the back stairs, or profess his love to her by singing "Georgia On My Mind." If she went downstairs, it invariably turned into an argument. She was fierce in her defense of family life, which to her did not include drinking of any kind. From the beginning, she had banished all alcohol to the outbuildings.

Downstairs, Mom often reprimanded Dad as we children lay tucked in our beds, suddenly afraid. Even our mild-mannered father was not always a predictable drinker and could spin like a car on ice, leading to instant danger. He was known for his physical prowess, and had left more than one man in his drunken wake. Once I heard my uncles speaking of a bully that Dad had thrown over the length of a car.

I do not remember him ever hurting Mom, only shoving her verbally when he was drunk, but my sister said that he slapped Mom once when she went downstairs in a flimsy nightgown, unaware that Dad had brought two drunken men home with him. It's easy to picture the men sitting sloppily in our kitchen rocking chairs, their youth long-lit and burnt and turned to ash, their glassy eyes caressing Mom's strong swimmer's body, and their lecherous leering too much for Dad to endure, even if they were his drinking buddies.

Sometimes when Dad returned home late, Mom let him call for her until he tired himself out singing, *Georgia, Georgia, the whole night through.* One very cold winter night he stopped singing and then started a fire in the living-room fireplace. In the early morning, I woke to Stephen rushing through the smoky upstairs hallway and hollering for us to all get up. Aubrey and I bucked from our beds like fawns, following Stephen and Mom downstairs.

The smoke was so dense that it gathered in our throats like seared moss. Dad had forgotten to open the flue and was passed out in a wooden captain's chair near the fireplace. His head was thrown back and his mouth was open, the smoke swirling around his face as if he had just wrestled a dragon. Looking at him, I guessed that Jack had not been nimble enough.

Dad was impossible to wake, so Stephen and I carried him outside and laid him like a dead man on the verandah. There was a dusting of snow and the rising sun lit the horizon pink. Mom quickly threw water on the smoldering fire in the fireplace and then followed us out. She pulled Aubrey to her side, pressing his red cheek against her flannel nightgown, both of them shivering, and all of us with trembling down-turned lips, waiting and praying for the drunken spell to be broken. Beneath the liquor curse was our loving father, the one who walked with us in the woods and rubbed our ears, the one who held us in his La-Z-Boy chair when we were brokenhearted. We'd learned long ago that the drinking father was just a lesser stand-in for our real one. Drunk, he could be funny, the one loose women sidled up to at the Legion Hall, begging him to dance, and men plastered him with free drinks just to hear him tell his stories of survival and mishap. How they must have howled with laughter, but we his family knew this understudy had not the soul for the part of our true father.

When Dad finally opened his eyes, they were bloodshot and wet as if he'd been crying in his sleep. He pulled himself up, using Stephen's shoulder as a crutch. He remained shaky, yet still for a moment, no doubt trying to figure out what had happened. He began to cough, and spittle laced with blood ran down his unshaven chin. He wiped it away with the back of his hand and then moved toward the door, touching each of us as he passed but saying nothing. His touch blossomed in us. I don't know what Mom was thinking, but I know we, his children, never adored him more. We accepted his waking as an answer to our prayers. Gathered together, we sipped his labored breathing like sweet juice. It trickled down our throats and quenched the singed moss.

Afterward, we raised all the windows and fanned the living room with folded newspapers. The newsprint stained our hands as if we had all reached into the fireplace and dipped them into a story of smoldering ash. *Ashes, ashes, we all fall down.* In years to come, I will associate the memory of our sooty fingers as the stain of our parents' bittersweet marriage, their discontent sometimes threatening us like a plague.

That day, our house inside felt colder than outdoors, and our breathing united in a cloud that mixed with the smell of oily smoke. Mom must have longed for her old love. All the things that she'd taken care of so lovingly were now silken with soot, even her children's lungs. What woman wouldn't have wanted a pilot to swoop in? What woman in this situation wouldn't have received an old love openly? Palm to palm, their aborted lifelines suddenly continuing on like a destined fault line, *And he walks with me, and he talks with me, and he tells me I am his own.*

Dad remained in his bedroom for the rest of the day, but his shape stayed on the verandah where we had laid him in the dusting of snow. How tall and thin it was. How desperate-looking, in the way he had slipped from our arms, so gangly. Nothing of his ropey strength showed. Staring at his outline, I know we children forgave him, our mercy lifting him up as if collectively it made a mossy forest floor beneath him.

I cannot speak for Mom, though. She had uttered only one thing that morning while fanning the smoke from the living room, *Hell on earth, it's hell on earth.* A dark cross-like smudge stained her heart-shaped forehead. The smudge was similar to the one some receive on Ash Wednesday. It didn't seem fair to me that she was the one always doing penance, the one cleaning up, the one praying, and for a moment I thought how nice it would be if she could go to the Legion Hall and dance her ass off. I pictured her that way, her face flushed and happy-looking, her hips wiggling and her fingers snapping.

———

On the day that Del and Mom visited in the strawberry field, I sat in the car watching them. I'd already concluded that Del was made up of both good manners and vanity. His slick brown eyes had left Mom for only a brief moment as he shook my hand. Then, I thought he was completely taken with her, but looking back, I think he was perhaps more taken with himself as he stood with his hands on his hips, broad-shouldered and grinning, the golden wings insignia on his American Airlines cap gleaming in the sun like a crown. It occurred to me then that he had practiced his presentation many times, like a man selling snake oil.

More than once while they visited, Mom tossed her hair and then tilted her head sideways. It was a youthful gesture. She had often confessed that in her heart and mind, she was forever eighteen, and that when she came upon her aged reflection in a mirror, it both startled and saddened her. Watching her, it seemed that she had traveled back and her youth was still a field waiting to be sprinted. All she need do was sip from the potion being offered.

In the morning heat, Mom's car smelled of leather and of the strawberries that I'd placed in the backseat. It also smelled of peppermint, which reminded me of Dad, who often freshened the mats with peppermint oil. Dad took care of things, lots of things. And if he couldn't organize or fix something, he found someone who could. Looking back, I suppose it was part of his penance for the drinking benders, or maybe it was simply that he loved Mom deeply. *Georgia on my mind.* Often, they touched and caressed one another. Watching, I imagined them massaging one another with a healing balm, something that wiped away all transgressions.

Watching Mom with Del, I wondered if her accidental rendezvous would make Dad jealous. Like most carousers, he could sometimes become unreasonably jealous. He'd seen and probably ventured too far on the nights that he stayed out late. When I became of legal age, he told me to stay away from the local drinking joint—*joint* being the operative word, one of his words that he used like a roadman's waving flag to signify possible danger. A local girl had been raped in the joint's bathroom. But since I knew that my drinking father sometimes went there himself, I challenged him. *Why should I stay away?*

Dad was leaning against the verandah railing smoking a cigarette and squinting at the hayfield. He had a worried look that was usually reserved for family. After blowing out a stream of smoke, he said, *Because girls have a lack of intention that men sometimes take advantage of. It's called innocence.*

I pictured the raped girl. Pretty, blonde, and wispy in nature, she now shuffled through the school hallways as if she were drugged, her glazed blue eyes looking forward, averting all human contact, and brimming with something that I couldn't quite define.

Still, I wondered if Mom would tell Dad about Del. And then I wondered if Mom's forever age was eighteen because she had been eighteen when she last saw Del. In one of his letters he had apologized for flying out on her birthday.

I recalled a scene from the summer, after the fireplace incident. Outwardly things had gone back to normal, but like the oily, smoky smell that lingered in our living room on damp days, a residue also seemed to linger on our parents, something alien and slippery that discouraged them from touching each other. Dad had not had a drink since the fire, nor would he ever again, but his lungs seemed weakened by the smoke, and an occasional gurgling cough haunted him. Haunted all of us, I suppose. What would we do without him?

The hayfield surrounding our house had just been cut by a nearby farmer and Aubrey and I were dragging the scratchy bales together to make a high pyramid. We'd been working for hours, for we knew the farmer would return the following day to trailer the bales to his barn. Each year, we built a higher and higher stack and then sat on the top bale as the sun set and the fireflies arrived, blinking and lighting up the sheared field all the way down to the creek.

We had just climbed up and were sitting together, sweating on the top single bale, when we heard the unusual roar of a low-flying plane. From a distance, it looked like the plane on the airmail envelopes. It was passing over the creek and coming toward us, spraying something that appeared to be foggy water. I imagined it coming to wash away the still-sooty smell in our living room or the slippery residue on our parents' skin. As it roared across the valley and over us, Aubrey and I stood and held our arms up, letting the moist spray land on us like a blessing. The setting sun made our dampened arms glow orange. When we turned to watch the plane go over our house, Mom rushed out, waving her arms as if she wanted the plane to land and rescue her. For a moment, she too was bathed in the foggy orange spray, and then seemed to disappear.

I tore down from the bales of hay and ran toward her. I thought that she had been abducted, zapped up by the spray, and my heart began to beat so hard that I could barely breathe. I imagined aliens with their fishbowl heads tying her to a bed in their plane while deciding which of her organs to harvest. Aubrey ran and panted behind me, no doubt thinking the very same thing. I reached back and grabbed his hand, squeezing it tightly, so he could keep up with me.

When we reached Mom, she dropped her arms down and hugged us to her chest. Her heart was beating hard and her chest rose and fell beneath our heads. She smelled of warm white cake, of vanilla, and she held us tightly for a very long time as if something bad had almost happened. When she finally let go, I saw that Aubrey's worried tears had left dirty streaks on her blouse. They looked like dripping soot. What would we do without her?

Just then Dad appeared on the verandah with the *Daily Gleaner* folded under his arm. The plane's engine could still be heard, but could no longer be seen. Dad said that the plane was spraying DDT to kill the budworms that were eating the spruce trees. He seemed pleased, and of course no one worried then about their families being bathed in pesticides. Such prescriptions were seen only as progress by Dad's generation, who prided themselves on taking care of things, never once suspecting that the beautiful place where we lived would eventually be dubbed Cancer Valley. I looked at the hills around us while noting that the crowns of the tall spruce trees had turned brown, and then Dad asked Mom if everything was all right, but I don't think she answered him. Instead, the question hung abandoned in the air between them.

After visiting with Del in the strawberry field, Mom got into the car. Del seemed to disappear as quickly as he had appeared, just as the spray plane had. Mom started her car and the new motor hummed. The radio was on low. *Doctor, doctor, give me the news, I've got a bad case of lovin' you.*

Mom snapped the radio off and turned to back away. Her face, which had looked so young only moments earlier, now looked as if she was in excruciating pain, as if something deep within her had been harvested. I thought of the word *excruciating*, and how it came from the Latin, meaning "out of the cross."

"Are you okay, Mom?"

"No. Yes." She chewed her lower crimson lip.

I wanted to ask what was wrong and I wanted to ask what she and Del had talked about, but I couldn't. By the look on her face, it seemed that she had come in contact with some sad truth that until then had only been suspected, or perhaps never even contemplated. For a moment, I thought of DDT. How now we all regretted being sprayed with it, but how at the time, it had appeared as a perfect poison, and then I thought how retrospect and regret often go together. I remembered the raped girl and I knew those were the emotions that lingered in her eyes as she shuffled through the school's hallways. Retrospect and Regret.

"What's he doing here?" I asked, realizing that the question sounded accusatory.

"Visiting an old friend."

"Is he married?"

"I didn't ask."

By then we were driving along the road that ran beside the railroad tracks. The same train that Mom and I often took to visit relatives traveled beside us, swaying and clacking. There was the smell of fresh-cut hay and of hot tar from a crew that was patching the road near the narrow black bridge. When we slowed down for the crew, a worker with whom I had gone to school waved and I waved back, inspiring his coworker to make a catcall. My friend swatted at the whistler and then looked at me and shrugged his shoulders. It was the same shrug he had given me once when we were both in grade six, and sitting at recess on the old fence behind our school. We had just finished our snack when he asked if he could kiss me. I looked at his fat lips, which were gleaming with potato chip grease. Okay, I said, immediately regretting the salty slug-like contact, the residue somehow soiling my innocence, although I could never have concluded that then.

Mom didn't seem to notice the workmen or the catcall. Her cheeks were flushed and her pained expression had now been exchanged for a puzzled one, as if she were trying to think something through, and even though we were very close and often intuitive regarding one another, I could not read her feelings. It was as if the encounter with Del had changed something between us.

"Are you going to tell Dad that you saw your old boyfriend?"

That question sounded accusatory, too, and I wished that I'd kept quiet.

"What good would it do?" Mom said, exasperated, as if some irreparable damage had taken place, something that Dad wouldn't possibly be able to fix.

What good would it do? I wondered then if even older women could be taken advantage of, because of their innocence.

Later that afternoon, Mom was sitting at the kitchen table writing in her journal. Her handwriting was forward-slanting and decorative. I could not decipher the words, but they looked like garland hung along a verandah. For her entire life, she'd been in the habit of writing letters and keeping diaries and journals. Mom loved words. I thought of all the lovely cards she had given to all of us, always with a note of how special we were, especially her cards to Dad.

What neither of us knew that day was that in a few years we would lose Dad, and a year after that Mom would suffer a stroke that would induce a severe and relentless case of logophilia. Arriving at her hospital room one morning, I will find her seat-belted in a chair with a fastened-on tray, and writing frantically on all the get-well cards that she's received. She will not look at me, or at any of my siblings when they arrive. She will not put her pencil down. She will not stop writing, word after word, phrase after phrase, written upside down and in circles, with ingenuity and zest: my siblings' names written randomly and then crossed out dozens of times, ditto with the salutations *dear* and *love*. And then the phrases: He is a Philanderer, We Drown by Shock, Small Price to Pay. Hope it's worth it. Dear, Dear, Dear, Love, Love, Love, Don't Drive, Please, Please, Please, I Saw the Doctor, Where Is Dad, Seep Off the Warm Wishes, Don't Sleep Alone, Please. Home Again, Home Again, Jiggity-Jig.

Disturbed by her sudden manic writing and large loopy letters, I will concentrate on her hands instead, the most recognizable part of her. I will recall her hands when I was a child. One morning after a surprise frost, I found a frozen hummingbird on the verandah. I was four and ran to Mom with it. She was washing the breakfast dishes, but quickly dried her hands on her apron and then laid the stiff red-throated bird in her palm, massaging its chest and wings. Her petting finger reflected the glistening morning sun. I was crying and she hushed me.

"Do you know, my little sweetheart, that this hummingbird's heart is twenty percent of its body weight?" She sang, *Wake my little darlin', Wake and see the sun.*

Within moments, the hummingbird opened its eyes and stood, cupped in Mom's glowing hands as if held in a nest of healing light. She continued to sing.

While recovering from her most severe stroke thus far, Mom will pass through several manic stages: repeating the same nursery rhymes over and over, insisting on walking around and around the perimeter of a room while touching and naming items: chair, painting, dresser, perfume, book, water glass, lamp, candle, tissues. And then later, she will enter a long period of mischievously repeating everything that she hears anyone say: I had a dream about you last night, Mom. *I had a dream about you last night, Mom.* We were picking strawberries. *We were picking strawberries.* You were back to your old self. *You were back to your old self.* Mmmm. *Mmmm.* Catching on to this, I said, You are my favorite child, both of us grinning as she promptly repeated, *You are my favorite child.* Yes, definitely. *Yes, definitely.*

Looking into her blue and satisfied eyes, I recalled what Flaubert's mother said to him—*Your mania for sentences has dried up your heart*—and how Robert Lowell rewrote the line, *Till the mania for phrases enlarged his heart.* And it seemed to me that *enlarged* was the right word. At least for Mom. Manically searching for words, she seemed immune from all the stroke had wrought. She seemed happy and childlike and free, and as odd as it might sound, after the first shock of seeing her so obsessed, it was a mysterious and beautiful thing to watch—Mom bigger than life, enlarged.

Even so, I was grateful when the mania passed.

Visiting Mom a few years later on her eighty-third birthday, I thankfully noted her recovery. I was thankful for Evangeline, too. Unable to face having Mom placed in a facility, no matter how effectively the facilitator sold the joint, she had arranged for Mom to live with her.

Mom still on occasion had a mini stroke, collapsing and stiffening like that frozen hummingbird, my tiny yet strong sister lifting and then encouraging her back to safety. Each time, Mom responded so beautifully to Evangeline's constant care that I had come to think of her caressing hands as healing hands, too, always glowing like Mom's had on the day that she revived the bird. *Wake my little darlin', wake and see the sun.*

On Mom's birthday, we were in her room at the nursing home where she would be staying for a few weeks to give Evangeline a rest. In the world of long-term caregiving, they call it a respite. Later that day, family would be coming for the birthday celebration, so I curled and combed Mom's hair and painted her fingernails with clear coat. As always, I begged to put a touch of my red lipstick on her, and as always, she said, "Absolutely not."

"When you die, I'll paint your lips red," I teased. "I'll paint you up just like a harlot."

Mom laughed and waved me off as she turned the blue swivel chair toward the window. The May sun made her ivory-colored dress that matched her skin gleam, and lit her white hair like a halo. She smiled looking out the window as if she were watching a rerun of her favorite movie, and then she reached for her notepad and began to write what I suppose was a note to herself.

While putting away the beauty supplies, I asked Mom how she now felt about seeing Del in the strawberry field. In my bag was the letter that I'd just received from my old boyfriend. I carried it with me just as I carried Mom's logophilia-inspired notes, as if they held a secret code.

Mom looked up from her notepad. I knew my face was no longer completely clear to her because of her failing eyesight, yet her gaze was intent.

"Well," she said, tilting her head, "at first, I regretted it, because he had seen an old woman. Now that was the way he would always remember me, not young and beautiful. But then after a while, the whole situation depressed me."

"Why?"

She looked down and began to draw a series of short vertical lines on the bottom of her notepad. They resembled a fence.

"He distracted me. And for a time, that was lovely. Oh, it was such a nice break from my housework and family things. I would do errands and housework without even realizing it. I think I must have wallpapered and painted every bedroom that year. It energized me, really." She looked up and smiled. "And it wasn't that I didn't love your father and my family. It was just that I didn't think about you all the time anymore. I thought of Del instead."

It was the first time that I'd ever heard her say his name, and she said it with such sweet submission that I smelled strawberries and heard the hymn that someone was humming in the field that day. *I come to the garden alone . . .*

Mom laid her pen on the writing pad and then casually crossed her arms.

"But after a while, I became very angry with myself. How I'd wasted so much time going over everything again and again, how excited I was to see him. It was silly romanticizing something that took place when I was a girl. By then, though, I was lost. I'd gotten out of the thought pattern for my own life and I couldn't get back to it. I couldn't find my way back."

"Is that what depressed you?" I asked.

"I guess." She sighed, clearing her throat. "You know what it was? My intuition was gone. And I didn't get it back for a very long time. That time was lost time. I don't believe in purgatory, but I suppose that might be what it would feel like. You know that you've lost something, but you don't know how to get it back. I regret it now, too. Especially the close time I lost with your father. I miss him so."

Mom turned her face to the brightly lit window again. A tear shimmered down her cheek, reminding me of the day she returned home with news of the horned doe.

I sat down and took her hand, which was soft and cool and as crepe-y as the paper of her old love letters.

"Don't be sad, Mom. Regret is lost time, too."

She took my hands and held them as if I were the one who needed comforting, or somehow needed to be revived. "I suppose it is," she said.

I passed Mom a tissue, and she wiped her nose and cheek.

"Thank you, dear."

Her room was quiet, and the sun was warm. The staff was cooking a birthday cake, and the scent of vanilla wafted through the hallway, smelling just as Mom had smelled on the day that the spray plane flew over. Down the hall, someone was listening to a Peter Gzowski interview on CBC radio. Sitting beside Mom in the sun reminded me of taking the train together when I was young. Those moments held such anticipation, and for a moment, I let myself believe that it was then, and we were on our way to visit loved ones.

"How did you find your way back, Mom? To Dad, I mean?"

"Oh," she said, "I made the choice to do it, and then I made it part of my routine. That's really what love is. Something that you do again and again, whether you feel like it or not."

Again and again. Is that what she had been trying to do with her random writing and repeating after her stroke? Get back to family?

Home again, home again, jiggity-jig.

The phone rang and Mom reached for it. Her sister was calling with birthday wishes and then family news, a breathy yes and a sigh, an *Mmm* and *Really*.

I moved to Mom's dresser and picked up a framed photo of her and Dad that had been taken the first year they were married. Dad stood behind Mom.

His stance was both strong and relaxed. One arm was wrapped around Mom's waist and she was clinging to his hand with both of hers, smiling so happily that it made me smile, too. When I was a child, the photograph had been mysteriously cut in two and lingered loosely with other odd photos in a shoebox. Now someone had glued it back together and put it in a silver frame, the cut looking like a barely visible scar from an incision. I thought how a ragged rip would have appeared more impulsive and less deliberate. I thought how sad the cut appeared, and then I thought how if it were Mom who had glued it back together, how difficult it must have been with her poor eyesight for her to get it so perfectly aligned. She must have attempted it again and again.

Mom hung up the telephone and when I glanced at her, she had a tinge of the same excruciating look that she'd had on the day that she returned to the car from the strawberry field. *Out of the cross.*

"Mom, do you have pain?"

She shook her head.

"What's wrong then?"

"I was thinking how I really do regret seeing Del again."

"Why?"

"Because I sinned," she said, self-assured, and then she cradled one palm in the other on her lap as if there lay something that she wanted me to see, but I saw nothing. The word *sinned* had taken me aback. I don't know why. I had grown up with it as a measuring stick for all that I did, but in that moment, it seemed archaic. I scrambled in my mind for a different word, a more digestible one, something that *Ladies' Home Journal* might use, but nothing came to mind. It occurred to me that perhaps there was no proper synonym for sin, and I promised myself to look it up later.

"How did you sin?" I asked.

"Oh," Mom said, closing her palms together, "I flirted with him. I did. And I felt guilty right away. But that isn't the worst part," she said. "The worst part was that after a few hours, I stopped feeling guilty and I started luxuriating in our meeting instead. Like I said, I overly romanticized it. I wasn't disciplined enough not to."

I noted the word *disciplined*, just as I noticed how frail Mom had become. She had lost weight and her shoulders were curving around her chest as if to protect her heart, that precious mother heart that she had flexed again and again for family. Surely, it was easily twenty percent of her body's weight. Her cheeks were hollow and her lips were held downward at the corners by age. In so many ways, her life had not been easy, and now it showed.

I remembered her on that morning in the smoke-filled house, *Hell on earth, it's hell on earth.* And how later, I had watched her carry the kindling from the fireplace box out to the shed, some of the twigs in her arms twisted up like broken antlers. I imagined her then as a rare horned doe that had just been defeated, a doe that had lost her horns of necessity, knocked from her like a crown in a battle.

"I think you're being too hard on yourself, Mom."

"I acted like a fool," she said.

"Mom," I said, laughing, "it's not like you got down and dirty with him in the strawberry patch."

"Deborah!" Mom tried to scold me but smiled instead, covering her mouth. Even though my risqué talk was the thing that she said I most needed to work on, I could still sometimes trick her with it and make her laugh, just as I suppose Del had tricked her with his easygoing charm.

"Really, Mom. It was a chance meeting with Del."

She looked at me, her blue eyes clear. "I'm not so sure it was."

"Really?"

She continued to look at me, but said nothing.

My mind scurried back to the day in the strawberry field. Del held no berry box to fill nor were his perfectly pressed khakis soiled from kneeling. He had simply appeared like a well-placed playing card. And Mom had said he was there to visit an old friend, but who was his old friend? My mother?

Just then Evangeline arrived with a stack of birthday gifts and a mass of mayflowers gathered with twine. Mom clasped her hands and smiled as Evangeline kissed her forehead, placing the flowers on Mom's lap. Mom picked the flowers up and held them the same way she had held them on the day she saw the doe with antlers. She held them like a bride.

Watching her, I wondered if her preoccupation with Del had not only taken her from her husband and intuition for a time, but also somehow from herself, from the girl in her. She'd been caught off guard, and perhaps even tricked, her heart momentarily changed by something unusual in the atmosphere. *Because girls have a lack of intention that men sometimes take advantage of. It's called innocence.* And there within, lay the graveness that I felt on that day she had been with Del in the field, her lack of intention, her lack of protective horns. I recalled asking her while driving away if she was going to tell Dad about meeting Del, and how perplexed I was when she said, What good would it do? Now it seemed clear that what she meant by that was that Dad wouldn't be able to fix it. What was done was done. Dad would have no healing balm for her feelings of regret.

I wanted to tell Mom that she was being too hard on herself, that one of her favorite hymns had accompanied her that day. *I come to the garden alone, while the dew is still on the roses.* I had read that the composer had in mind Mary Magdalene's moments with the risen Christ. His followers questioned him when he forgave her, but I have to think he saw through her so-called sin to the beauty of it, saw that perhaps at times her sensuality was the most magnificent thing she had to offer. Was this not his ultimate talent? That he received all? And did Christ not defend Mary Magdalene by saying, She has loved many. Did he not defend her for what the world has deemed to be her greatest sin? If that were so, how easy it must have been for him to forgive my mother if need be. After all, she'd only flirted with an old boyfriend.

Instantly I was infuriated with Del, his reappearance and his accusatory good-girl comment from long ago. How dare he judge my mother for marrying my father? Suddenly, I felt sorrow for Mom. Sorrow, for her having been judged.

Looking back later, I will also feel sorrow for myself. I knew that both Mom and I were women like so many others, always measuring ourselves by the yardstick of sin and always trying to be good girls. It seemed that I was never without the conflict of it. In one of the family photo albums, there was a picture of me at the age of four, standing in the hayfield in front of our home. I wore a perfectly pressed sundress with a bow at the back, my hair in a high ponytail with a bow as well, and I was looking down at something in my hands. Beneath the photograph, Mom had written, *He Loves Me, He Loves Me Not*, signifying that it must have been a daisy in my hands. Studying the photograph closely, I see an introspective child, one already worried about being good and pleasing to my mother and to God, and sometimes they blended into one. *He loves me, He loves me not. She loves me, She loves me not.*

———

A few weeks after Mom's very last birthday, I sat before my dressing-table mirror, painting my lips red. Outside, the warm June sun simmered honey from the lilacs. If I were to go through with my accepted lunch date the following day, my old boyfriend would also see someone much older than he remembered. I would not be the girl he'd met when I was eighteen. Suddenly, I had the urge to call Mom, but didn't. I knew if I confessed the invitation, she would tell me not to go. Besides, I reasoned, I'd already confessed the invitation to my husband, and he had agreed for me to see it through.

That day I left for the garden center without the slightest worry, even though looking back now, there were signs. I left my husband weeding and our daughters building a fairy house under a maple sapling in the backyard. In their play, the fairies they build homes for are always orphans, stranded without parents and left to start a new life. They return over and over to this scenario just as I did as a child. It was the thing I, too, feared most: being orphaned.

Where was my intuition then?

I bought bright purple irises with yellow centers, white rhododendrons, pink azaleas, and variegated hosta, all in a sea of sappy preoccupation. I was thinking of my old love, of course, thus the adrenaline high. Thus the interpretation of feverish summer heat in my bedroom and thus, no doubt, the painting of the lips of the bust red. I would never have admitted this then, but I was in that state when the first contemplation of sin, or offense or transgression or peccadillo, is aligning itself with the beguiling justification that one must be true to one's feelings. It was no doubt the very state Mom had confessed to luxuriating in, the state that had caused her to eventually become so depressed. *Doctor, doctor, give me the news. I got a bad case of lovin' you.*

Still, I wondered, what woman who has been married for twenty years does not welcome this guided imagery, if only for a moment while she folds another load of laundry or stands with her hands in tepid dishwater?

———

His letter also recalled the golden lit windows of my family's rambling home as he pulled into my driveway that first night, smoke twisting from the twin chimneys, and the way I said *See ya 'round*, and then the way I turned before stepping inside the house and waved, pink-gloved fingers splaying like a fan. And how the confetti snow remained on the floor of his car for days, and how much later when all the snow was gone and it was spring and then summer, he saw me at the local five-and-dime and I invited him for Sunday dinner with that same expectant smile he'd been thinking about all winter and spring, and hadn't been able to forget, although he'd wanted to, because he was so much older.

And after Sunday dinner, how my family gathered on the benches and in the rocking chairs on the long verandah and talked while looking out to the hayfield that had just been cut and he breathed the sweet hay, and how that sealed him to me, that fresh smell, preserved by the sound of the screen door whining open and closed, and the sounds of voices, particularly Mom's, which he said was like a siren's song, not lamenting, he said, but enchanting. And he loved so much a family coming and going, dinner cooking, a long table being set, grace being said. You wore your father's straw fedora that evening on the verandah, do you remember?

No, although I wanted to.

That day at the garden center, I moved through the hot rows of plants, breathing in the sickly sweet aroma of too many things in bloom, filling my wagon with one plant and then another, and finding decisions impossible to make. Why not take them all? Why not have it all? Something in bloom, and something about to bloom again?

In that moment, I coveted my guided imagery like a crow with a stolen button in her beak. When I caught my passing reflection, I barely recognized myself, a banshee, a vague yet familiar shape running toward me in a dream. What else did he remember of me? Me, Me. My mind buzzed. I pictured the night pasture lit and glittering, as if it held a million fireflies.

I believed Mom's regret about seeing Del again. I believed as Marguerite Duras had written, that fidelity was the sexiest thing to be had, this from a woman who wrote *The Lover* and had her own erotic experiences to draw from. Who was I to question her? Who was I to question the wisdom of my mother? Of God?

Yet, his letter had presented such enticing memories, inspiring feelings that I knew were consuming me with sentimentality. And my husband didn't even carouse. I entertained my thoughts anyway, securing youthful images of myself like treasures woven into a nest. Acting like a fool.

Part Three

one

*A*nother wooden beauty, the sailboat *Capri* is being launched just as the poet Philip Booth and his wife Margaret arrive on the town dock. I have not seen them since last fall, longtime year-rounders who became summer residents because of need, slipping away last October for Hanover, New Hampshire, and conspicuously absent for the white barren months.

The Booths were here when we arrived in Castine, and for generations before that. Margaret is a strong Southern woman with wonderful manners that allow everyone dignity, and this is what Philip is being allowed as he maneuvers through the early stages of Alzheimer's. Dignity was also what Margaret allowed me when I was nine months pregnant with Phoebe. While some were saying *Haven't you had that baby yet,* she while passing me on the sidewalk near the post office, simply said, *You must feel wonderful, because you look wonderful.* No questions or accusations, an encouragement wrapped in good manners that endeared her to me forever. I was big, bloated, and tired, but her statement made me lift my chin, made me believe I could make it to delivery, which, as it turned out, was only hours away.

When we first arrived, Philip put my family at ease, too, staying back at first like any local, and then coming closer. Over the years, he has hugged my daughters, bought them impromptu ice-cream cones at the Variety, twisted his worn baseball hat on backwards and made faces until they howled with laughter. He has danced with them at Dennett's restaurant, letting them twirl like princesses beneath him. In other words, he has given them a wide berth to be free, just as he has given me, always speaking as a comrade, but never crowding with writerly advice.

Part of me is tempted to run and greet the Booths, but my voyeur side wins out. Watching without involvement may be the ultimate for any writer. Nothing can be ruined that way. You get to think whatever you want, to imagine the conversation that in one way will never take place, and in another way, already has. I assume this is what Emily Dickinson experienced watching and recording from the comfort of her home. This is what she meant by *a certain slant of light.*

The Booths lean over the pier's railing, watching the young couple adjust the ropes on *Capri.* I wonder what Philip is thinking, or trying to remember. Maybe the lines from the poem he wrote about Eaton's Boatyard are with him now, tethered as anything dear might be. For years, he strolled from their gracious home on Main Street—the home that anchors all those generations to the harbor—taking in details with clarity and regard, the same way he seems to be taking in minutiae now. I wonder if he knew in those days of razor-sharp thinking that he would be here this twelfth day of June, perhaps remembering what he can no longer say, or maybe feeling the things that scarred his palms so long ago . . . *to forget for good all the old year's losses, save for what needs to be retrieved: a life given to how today feels: to make of what's here what has to be made to make do.*

Philip walks east toward the Breeze takeout and the Maine Maritime dock where training boats are gathered and tied, much larger than anything else now that the behemoth training ship has left for its summer excursion. When *The State of Maine* hugs its dock in the winter, these tugs and research vessels look playfully small, but now they take on a presence of their own, almost stately, reminding me how the locals come out of the shadows after the summer people leave, and how majestic they appear when not in the shade of newcomers.

Philip's hands are relaxed in his khaki pockets, his green button-down shirt is worn, adopting the shape of his recently acquired round belly. Beneath his faded baseball cap, he looks this way and that, taking in all the details— stopping, looking, listening—the salty air and warm sun no doubt stirring words and phrases. Even if they are tied in his mind too tightly now, they remain present. This morning, Philip is every bit the literary diplomat, the caption of that ever-pending poem, moving toward things more distant, while Margaret floats behind, not his dinghy in any way, just partnered now more than ever, following him on to deeper waters. *Following*, that transitive verb that can mean "to obey or to go along," but in their case clearly means "to accompany: to go together."

Watching them makes me miss Bill, who left for the West Coast a week ago. A dear friend's young daughter drowned. John Blackwell is a powerful and sensitive drummer, who once said that all the musical notes in his head were color-coded. Synesthesia. I cannot help but wonder if his daughter's death will have its own color-coded note now. Surely, some deaths pull even tighter than the death of a mother and a father, a rope that lassos and constricts one's organs forever, distress, misery, grief, and woe. And what, Mother of God, would the color be for such gangrene? The blackness of a deep dark hole. *A Blackwell.*

Later today, Bill will return, but it will be tomorrow before we really have time together, for he has made a habit of first spending time with our daughters. This serves them well. They have grown confident in expecting their father's love, and it serves me well, too, for I only grow more attracted to him as he bestows his care and attention on them. If Marguerite Duras is right and fidelity to one's partner is the sexiest thing to be had, then fidelity to one's family may run a close second.

Kenny Eaton is back with the man that he convinced to do the launching, unloading a huge motorboat, *Semper Fi*. As I suspected, Always Loyal. She is unloaded quickly and efficiently without much of an audience. The midmorning brings a less attentive crowd. A boat is a boat is a boat, just as a seagull is a seagull, and the tide is the tide. Most are vacationing and do not have time for the finer details, just the long sweeping view before they have to leave. Back home, their minds may recall this small coastal village as if they are flipping through a pile of similar postcards.

Sliding into the water, *Semper Fi* makes a loud white splash. Before she is turned about, Kenny speeds up over the hill to Main Street where he will probably park his truck and trailer illegally beside the Variety. The parking spaces are gone now, used up by the less attentive, those who drift in to sample it all, but to know none of it, not because they are not capable or wouldn't like to, but because they don't have time, or perhaps as children, they were victims of curtained rooms and afternoons of television, or perhaps their schedules were jammed with one lesson after another, no time for pollywogs. Now, they guard themselves with sun hats and sunglasses, cell phones and designer tote bags. All of that would have to be left behind for them to be led by the day.

At the Variety, Kenny will grab a coffee to go, while having several quick and clipped conversations—no need to enunciate when you are in a rush. Let's just get on with it. I've got a million things to do today.

———

Last night, I dreamt that I stood naked on the sail loft's deck. Standing before a full moon, so emptied, feeling that my legs and arms felt useless, heavy yet also light, as if they were made of driftwood and I had floated on a cold numbing sea. The waves beneath the deck began to swell and swirl as if some creature were spinning beneath them. For a moment, a sail as thin as worn gossamer appeared, and on it was a map in sepia, its edges dotted with horned dragons. The deck began to rock and the cloth blew up like a bellying sail. I tried to grab it, but tumbled into the waves instead, the warm murky water churning me like butter.

I woke terrified, panting, the bed damp and my lips tasting of sea salt. Reaching for Bill, I realized that he wasn't there. But today the dream's terror is gone—a dream is a dream is a dream. I breathe deeply, filling my lungs with salty air, and then emptying them. For the first time in a very long time, I feel an attachment taking shape, not only to Jinx, who is standing on a buoy in the distance, drying his wings, but to the world that holds this bird. So much since Mom's death has registered on the same dull barometer, my heart barely beating in its mournful hibernation.

Anne of Castine and her captain motor north past the sail loft, the tiller lightly held—no need to live in chronos here—the tethered wooden dinghy cutting a whisper through the sunlit water. *Anne* is quiet as she moves, as if propelled by some force other than her motor, some whispering encouragement coming from beneath the sea. Maybe this is something that great boatbuilders understand, a spark that they try to ignite while cutting and sanding and polishing, some friendly dragon that they hope to wake.

The *Capri* couple watches *Anne*, as do several others. Even a few of the inattentive are suddenly captivated. Maybe this is the sight that will ignite something in one or more of them as they flip through their memory photos back home. Some may venture back to Castine, and one or two may become regular visitors, or summer renters or summer people with their own homes, or eventually year-rounders, like me.

While *Anne*'s owner holds her tiller lightly, she makes a hissing, kissing path through the water, not seeming to care if people even know she exists. Within seconds, she whispers out of sight, *Know me.*

———————

I found the ad for the sail loft while sitting at the Fishnet in Blue Hill, eating fish chowder with my daughters, and reading the want ads in the local newspaper. It was May and sunny, but cold and windy, and I was not looking for a place to rent for the summer, even though I had rented several places for writing over the years. Winter was the time I'd always chosen to rent—the second floor of the post office, a small cottage overlooking the yacht club, and a few times, a cozy house on Green Street that belonged to dear friends from California. *Please use our house. We'll never come in the winter. Never.*

As for real estate on that cold May day, I was obsessing on a sprawling Nantucket-like house for sale on up the Bagaduce River, but still in the village. A place with a field at the water's edge where lupines and sea roses grew, a place for daughters to be married and dance, a place with a private writer's nook tucked high in the eaves, a place owned by older friends who were planning to join the Booths in New Hampshire. A house I not only liked, but had a desire to take over, because I liked the owners, they, too, having lovely manners.

We had reached an agreeable price. All we needed to do was to sell our house. For days before Bill left for California, we had been in a lockdown cleanup, getting-our-house-ready-to-show mode. One of the few Victorian houses in the village, it has an inviting front porch and small rooms with high ceilings that make it both cozy and occasionally elegant. When we moved from Massachusetts, we had stripped it to the rafters, replacing the wiring, the plumbing, the roof, ceilings, walls, fireplaces, sidings, and windows. We built a new kitchen and added showers and soaking tubs in the bathrooms. A crew sanded and painted the walls the color of butter. More recently, we'd gutted the three bedrooms on the third floor, creating a white loft space where Bill works when he is not on the road for his family business. From a long line of cymbal makers dating back to 1623 in Turkey, his last name, Zildjian, means son of a cymbal maker.

Bill loves our home's proximity to the village. Within a few minutes, we can reach our daughters' school, the post office, T&C grocer, the Compass Rose Bookstore, Bah's Bakehouse, the Variety Store, Four Flags, Trinity Church, and the town dock, where we keep our battered skiff. Often a summer's evening walk has ended with dinner at the Castine Inn or the Pentagoet, the Harbor Lodge or Dennett's, or the Manor Inn on Battle Avenue.

Moving to the Allens' property would take us farther away from Main Street, but it is our Japanese garden that Bill would find hardest to leave. When news of September 11 came, he and the landscapers were rolling in boulders the size of huddled people. Since, the garden had bonded him to our property, and that is where I find him in his spare time, transplanting moss, clipping and sweeping. That is where he received the news of Mom's death, and it is where he goes when hearing other bad or disappointing news.

From the kitchen window, I often watch him as he kneels to sweep cultch from the moss at the edge of the *tsukubai*, his hair appearing to be the jet black it was when we married, even though it's now more salt than pepper. Still, as he kneels, it appears black, as if by submitting to the garden, he is young again. The poet Patrick Lane wrote, "The gardener is made young by the seasons as they turn." Indeed.

The garden is Bill's parterre in every way, designed as a series of rooms: a kata room with a *shishi-odoshi*, to scare the deer at its edge; a *tsukubai*, which is a giant rock with a hollowed-out basin for washing one's hands before entering the shed teahouse; a tiny raking sand garden surrounded by lowbush blueberries for the girls to harvest; a garden path lined with clumps of moss that resemble a family of raccoons; and an area with glittering stones—a gray stone with the word FAITH carved across it, a sparkling hunk of pink granite placed in memory of Mom, and an iridescent stone to remind me of the pool green of Dad's eyes.

Washing dishes, I often watch Bill in the garden kata room, doing karate in his white gi. As a black belt, he knows twenty-six katas, each a series of ancient fight moves that have trained him to react instinctively in self-defense. His heavy cotton gi is as crisp-looking as his moves, which are quick and clean and powerful. Second only to his good looks and manners, it was his physical strength that attracted me in the beginning. Just back from rock climbing in Yosemite National Park, he was working in the foundry of the family business. Day after day, he lifted heavy molten bronze and poured it into the cymbal molds, using a secret process that his Armenian ancestors had followed for over a thousand years, starting with an alchemist who worked for the sultan. His work routine had left him as cut as any prizefighter. On one of our first winter walks through a grove of birch trees in the New Brunswick woods, he lifted me onto a high rock to view a frozen waterfall, and it was as if he were lifting nothing. With his hands snug around my waist, I knew I could trust him, knew that he would not touch me, nor anyone else, unnecessarily.

Later, I learned that he could go without food and sleep and still be energetic, something I assume he inherited from his other ancestors, who were Scottish Highlanders. Despite his Scottish and Armenian heritage, though, he is most comfortable with Japanese culture and its tradition of etiquette. In a family business with a narcissistic patriarch, and siblings who, like The Two Bitches in *Aesop's Fables*, think that having a thing is more important than having the right to it, the rules of ancient culture have been a sanctuary for him. No wonder his hair turns back to black when he kneels in the garden. No wonder he nurtures this place of rock and moss. He once said, Nature hates a garden, and the essence of one is man's attempt to create order from chaos. He went on to say that karate was an attempt to create order from the chaos of combat.

"Yes," I said, "and writing is an attempt to create order from one's life."

"That makes sense." He smiled.

Still fully aware of Bill's contentment, I had him in the clutches of yet another real estate possibility, an activity he endures with patience. I often wonder why I, the restless one, ask that he give up his contentment. Little have I known that it was not a different home that I needed, but an escape from domesticity, just as Mom had suggested. *You write too well to do housework.*

I needed a place to dream and to remember, a place to align myself with the past, so that I might align myself with the cormorant. Anne Morrow Lindbergh wrote, "When one is a stranger to oneself then one is estranged from others, too, the wilderness stretching out between you."

two

*W*hen I wake from a nap on the linen sofa, clouds are hording on the horizon and the noontime wind has picked up, making the halyards clang. The sun is blinding and the sea-churned air smells like the trail along a sandy dune. To breathe deeply is to be present with all the beaches that I've ever loved, to see a thousand shades of silky sand, to feel grimy warmth so intensely that it creates a noun as adequate as any organ. *Dunicity.*

The weather in the sail loft is ever changing yet always as concentrated as bouillon. On damp days, I start a fire, which always smokes, the wind shoving the smoke back down the chimney like a cover slammed shut on an urn.

Breathing in wisps and tinges of smoky residue, I listen to the rumbling *woo*, the circling howl, the clanging halyards, still sleepy from the atmospheric melody. It's been my favorite anesthesia since Bill and I sailed on Massachusetts Bay as newlyweds. Once during a particularly gusty gale, he reassured me that all he need do was pay attention to the sails. Reassured, I fell asleep, leaving him to man the sailboat on his own. It is a story he sometimes tells. Not critically as some men might, but endearingly, which is the way he approaches our history together.

"I kept calling for her to wake up," he'll say. "I was afraid she'd roll from the boat." His brown eyes are yielding when he says the word *afraid*. Yet it is not weakness that appears, but a vulnerable strength, as if *afraid* is a place within him just as endurance is. A place he has honed. Afraid is a muscle that he has flexed over and over. Afraid meanders like a worn path through his pasture. Early in our marriage when I hemorrhaged with a bleeding ulcer, he never left my side, staying with me for days after I returned home from the hospital, even though he was scheduled for a business trip to Europe.

Go, I said.

We were in our bedroom in an apartment in an old weathered mansion on the South Shore of Boston. The winds were howling. Once the servant quarters, the rooms were nestled high in the eaves like a nest, and even on the most blustery days, one felt hidden like a pearl within a shell. Bill's suitcases sat beside the bedroom door and he was standing near the multipaned window in front of our bed, watching the sun rise over the sea. The water was cerulean with forceful whitecaps, each rising like a pirate's hook.

He stood with his hands in the pockets of his dark suit pants, rattling coins, a habit of all the men that I've ever loved. He had not put his suit jacket on and his well-defined muscles showed through his white oxford shirt, the way the shape of a rock might show through a drying beach towel. The rising sun cast his shadow on the wheat-colored coverlet and his shape lay over me. Like the potter's daughter, I traced my lover's outline, picturing him as a Scottish Highlander, as unlikely a fit for this world as any constant traveler might be, clinging to his cloak as the winds blew, when all he really wanted was to be warmed by the sun.

"Billy, I'm okay. You can go."

"I'm afraid," he said, turning from the window. He came and sat on the end of the bed and rubbed my feet beneath the coverlet. His black hair glistened.

"Of what?" I asked.

"Of losing you." His eyes were a deeper brown than any freshly tilled and lush earth. They glittered as if dusted with mica. I knew his father would criticize him if he remained home, knew that it would be added to the long list of unfair judgments. To such a father, a son's autonomy is always a sin.

"Then stay." I smiled.

He crawled in beside me. The persistent wind rattled the windowpanes and sighed through the room. His shirt was taut and smooth against my cheek and smelled of freshly pressed starch. He smelled of ancient spices: cinnamon and cardamom and mint. In my mind, I pictured him as having traveled a great distance toward me. Years later, while reading a Donald Hall poem, I would be reminded of that windy day we spent in our bed together, *What overflowing comfort as we rose and fell in the body's restitution.*

My ulcer never bled again.

The town parking lot is filling with cars as tourists arrive to lunch at Dennett's. At high noon, few locals are patrons of the restaurant, but in the evening, the long bar will fill with local faces and summer visitors returning, and the occasional migrant sailor. Most sailors appear uninterested in the motley crew, but once or twice, I've seen one with eyes as shiny as mirrors, probably from too much alcohol, but I always like to think the reflection bores from their very center, as all wishes do. Their eyes glitter to attract attention, a story, a memory ignited, a warm and soon to be naked body, restitution, healing.

An obese lady steps from her car only to have her floppy straw sun hat stolen by the wind. For a time, she hobbles after it, but the hat is like a puppy being released from its tether, first going this way and then that. The lady is awkward, her wide bottom as fluid as a jellyfish beneath her peach shorts. Soon some townie children join in, chasing the floppy hat, but it is not long before the hat lifts and blows straight out to the bay as if that were its intention all along. To escape. It soars like a toy parachute, the ones attached to tiny plastic soldiers. The woman turns to her husband—her mouth hanging open in disbelief—a large man still standing beside their car. He shrugs. His pants are suspended as if he had recently been parachuted and dropped from the sky himself.

The woman looks around the parking lot as if searching for help, anyone, a dock attendant, a parking attendant, a police officer, but she will find none of that here. This is a village that exists without much official support. Few tourists or newcomers understand that for it to remain charming, it must be run somewhat lawlessly. Few understand the importance of leaving the old waterfront buildings lopsided and dingy. From a distance, they are like dusty wooden toys thrown in a pile. Up close, they are a multitude of treasures. When one is purchased and renovated, the locals mourn.

The couple hobble together and then walk toward Dennett's, their eyes downcast on the pinkish gravel road, their features appearing to be held in a droopy pectin that I suspect is disappointment. Days and years of life not going the way they both had hoped, their dreams now lacking resilience, marching behind them like tired soldiers. Dream-soldiers who were once young, no doubt walking so straight that it seemed a solid wooden cross was stitched within their chests. Now their bodies sag, yet they move steadily, more from habit than conviction, their crosses having finally turned to cinders like trees after a fire.

———

Heading toward Eaton's Boatyard, Max and I face the warm blustery wind. As we pass Dennett's, the wind begins to set a steadier course from the northeast, instantly washing away the smell of fried fish and french fries. The restaurant is fat with the visiting lunch crowd. If I had been dropped into this scene, the wind-muffled roaring of patrons might easily be deciphered as alarm, a ship keeling sideways with passengers beginning to panic. I imagine the overweight couple amidst it, mute and witnessing, their appetites momentarily exhausted from overeating, their eyes damp and noncommunicating. Excommunicated from the world years ago by those haunting disillusioned soldiers that follow them, the couple sit at the edge of life's basin—strangers to themselves and to one another—never daring to lean forward and sip, even when circumstance tips them in an encouraging way, their dismal routine having stolen their impromptu lives away.

I recall the man's hand held behind his wife's back, floating lightly above her swinging arse as they passed the sail loft, his hand like a small bird trying to land on a wayward child. It seemed that he too was suffering the loss of that hat. Why had she worn that hat? Did she think within its flopping shade she would appear thinner? Or was the hat an affectation, something that marked their yearly escape to the seashore? Had it sat in an overstuffed closet all winter, waiting? Had their dog been tempted to chew it, or had a grown daughter, threatened with inheriting her parents' parade of defeat, been tempted to stuff it into the trash? The disappointment on her face still a reflection rather than a weight, a splash rather than a stain, something that could still be rinsed away, if only she were brave enough to sip from the world's basin. Will she? Will she overcome their routine of defeat?

Max hugs my ankles as we near the tiny beach just past Dennett's, which is his mannerly way of saying that he'd like to stop. There, on the damp sand, his tiny footprints will remain like fossils until the tide rushes in, my barefoot markings beside them. He squats to relieve himself and then chases two terns. Compared to him, running and jumping, the birds are no more than pencil dashes. He is a flamboyant paragraph I read over and over, but never tire of. He, with his rusty soft locks, who is in love with the sun and the seashore and me. So much so that when he dies, I will collect the lacy coffin-box bryozoans that gather on the kelp and wrap him in it. I will hold him like a baby. Then, I will give him and his floppy-ear story to the sea. The perfect paragraph floating away.

The pay phone outside the boatyard office is ringing. It hangs on the lower end of the narrow, two-story, shingled shanty, which was once an abandoned chicken coop on that opposite shore. After coming loose in a storm, it was salvaged by Kenny. The telephone ringer is on a speaker, and the shrill sound vibrates on the wind and then dissipates like a woman's scream. Who calls a pay phone? A mother, a lover, a daughter, a child? No one ever seems to answer the ringing phone, and although I am often tempted, I never do, imagining my own desperate voice on the other end, lost in orbit since the day Mom died. *Wait—not yet, Mom. I'm not ready.*

What would I ask Mom if I could speak to her again? I would ask about the Cannered Noz, a tale that she told me not long before she died: diminutive elderly peasant women who inhabit shallows of rivers and stony banks. Mom said at night they could be heard washing the linen of humans dying without absolution. It was the word *absolution* that stayed with me, first floating like a feather the way she said it so softly, blown like a farewell kiss—*absolution*—but also with a hint of the powerful hiss of waves. What did the Cannered Noz sound like? Like the sizzle of the sea on a hot beach? Cloth against a washboard? Humming? Chanting? An outcry? I knew the tale was told, as all her tales were, to instruct. Absolution. What did it sound like? What did it feel like? Mom must have wanted me to know.

———

Eaton's long ramshackle boathouse stores sails and masts and hovers over the tides just as my rented sail loft does. I step through the heavy slider door out of the wind, letting my eyes adjust to the cool darkness. Slowly, the interior of the ravaged building reveals itself. Like a buried treasure, it smells of having been in wet sand, hidden for years at the bottom of the sea. It seeps dunicity. Erected in 1890, it has been a salt shed, a lumberyard, a stable, and a creamery, and since 1939, a boatyard belonging to the Eaton family.

Following Kenny up steep stairs to the second story last week and stepping over a hole in the floor big enough for a giant to slip through—he called it the hellhole—I felt as if I were being led through a surreptitious mortuary. There, small dusty engines shaped like hearts and an assortment of black corroded iron organs lay, dusty wooden trunks and bound mildewed sails tagged with the white tags of autopsy. Cardboard boxes, damp and beginning to collapse like an abandoned honeycomb, were stacked along one wall, some with sticky-looking stains.

Studying the boxes, I felt overcome. After the death of each of my parents, it had occurred to me that in the end, their lives had been reduced to a box. While each of their bodies were carried away in a large ornate wooden box, what remained of their lives was eventually preserved in a smaller box: a few documents, a will, and a stack of cherished correspondence and photos, the larger possessions having all floated into the nets of family members or to the auction house.

"Whoa, Kenny. What's in all these boxes?"

"Stuff that belongs to other people. Stuff from boats."

"What people?"

"Mostly people who are gone now."

By his downward glance, I knew that he didn't mean people who had departed on boats, but rather those who had already been wrapped in coffin lace by their loved ones. Who knew what seas they now floated on.

"Why do you keep their stuff?"

"Why shouldn't I?"

His eyes brightened like a boy's. Of course, he had a tenable argument. And I knew better than to challenge him, for it is when he is at his most boy-like that Kenny can turn as gruff as a ram. He leaped over a pile of coiled ropes.

"People always think they'll come back. If they don't, sometimes someone in their family does."

Of course. And here the sweet evidence was stacked. Their lives had existed. Their loved one had not only passed through, but still occupied a space in this place, like sap seeping from the boards of a wrecked ship, the distress flag still flying, albeit faintly. Here someone could come and touch their loved one's condensation, press it to their lips, feel it stick.

"Anything here you want?" Kenny asked.

I looked around, pleased, but trying not to show it, having learned that the trick with a hard-core local was to treat them with the same disinterest with which they often treated you. The mystery boxes appealed to me, but which one would I take? And what if someone eventually came looking for the box that I had chosen? Or what if within the possessions I chose, I found a responsibility, a note or a message that needed to be delivered?

"I know," Kenny said. He walked to one corner.

I thought he was heading toward a dusty blue tarp that seemed to hide a huddled woman, her spine curving like a bow, but instead he grabbed a broken lobster crate, reached within, and pulled out a decaying net that held a green glass buoy.

"You can have this." As he held the net high, a shard of sunlight poured through the broken window and lit the buoy, reflecting a crack the color of fire. The eye of a dragon. "My father left this here."

He rolled the net and then walked toward me. "Now, you can't say I never gave you nothin'."

I smiled, accepting the gift as a token of his momentary acceptance of me, but maybe he was simply trying to get rid of me. *I've got a million things to do today.*

Leaving, I asked Kenny why he called the hole in the floor the hellhole.

"Because someday someone is going to fall through it and break their damn neck. Kids come up here at night. When I catch them, I tell them I'll ram every one of them down that hole if they get up here again, but they always come back." He looked at me with what I could only interpret as anger. "They don't listen."

I stood looking down through the hole. It was a long distance to the floor below.

"Why don't you fix it?" I asked.

"Can't fix everything," Kenny said, rushing toward the stairs. It was nearing the end of the day and he was beginning to limp.

It occurred to me then that Kenny might be a man who had accepted that fact long ago. A person couldn't fix everything, but they could do their best to fix the things that absolutely needed it. *Save for what needs to be retrieved.*

I turned and looked at the honeycomb of belongings, the blue tarp covering whatever or whomever lay there, the pyramid of old paint cans, and then I turned and jumped over the hellhole just as Kenny had.

Leaving the boatyard with the bundled net, I noted some of the things that needed to be fixed: the door hanging crooked on the pirated chicken coop, a boat trailer with two flat tires, several broken sawhorses, the third wooden step on the steep stairway that led to Water Street. Heading home in the dark two nights ago, I'd forgotten about it, gouging my calf on a twisted nail as my foot fell through the broken step. I had since memorized its location the same way I suppose Kenny had memorized his footing in the attic.

The third step, the third step.

Walking between the masts with Max, I find Kenny's daughter Suzanne near the front of the building. She is shelling lobsters that smell of sea musk and penetrable salt, the kind that the sun dries in the cracks of one's body after swimming in the sea for hours. If the sun catches a salt-laden body just right, it appears to be encrusted with diamond flecks. The cracked and piled coral lobster shells are stunning. Nothing should look this alive when it is dead. A sheath, a shell, a carapace, worthy of lamenting.

Suzanne is the only woman who works at the boatyard. Her stance is low and solid, suggesting anchoring, and her shield strong enough to reflect her father's sudden bursts of temper or short-lived sulky silences. Her questioning look can dissolve the advances of surly sailors as if they are simply schoolboys reaching their hands out for a cracker. Witnessing this, I often think of those lines from Yeats. *The half-read wisdom of daemonic images, Suffice the ageing man as once the growing boy.*

Suzanne snaps a lobster tail and then pushes the moist and plump meat out.

"Having lunch?" I ask.

"No." She grins. "I'm sick of them. We've got a yacht coming in, and the captain ordered twenty pounds, shelled."

"Oh, that's why no one is around."

She grins again. Her brown hair is cropped in a bob, her lips so sun-shredded that they will stay pinkish-white all winter long, the pinkish-white of mayflowers and of tears in a young girl's eyes. Suzanne's appealing square-shaped fingers are smeared and shiny with lobster juice. Her hands are shaped exactly like her mother's, who was the first person to welcome me to Castine. A fellow Canadian from Cape Breton, we immediately landed on our shared affection for Alistair MacLeod's writing, recalling his work as fervidly as Cannered Noz scrubbing their prayers into linens:

In the early madness of the lobster season they did not speak to one another although they saw each other almost every day. The men were often up at three in the morning brewing their tea by the flickering lamps, casting their large shadows eerily upon the shanties' walls as they moved about in the semidarkness. At night they sometimes fell asleep by eight. Sometimes still sitting on their chairs, their heads tilting suddenly forward or backward and their mouths dropping open. She worked with her mother, planting the garden and the potatoes. Sometimes in the evening she would walk down by the shanties, but not very often. Not because she felt uncomfortable walking so close to so many men. Sometimes they nodded and smiled as all of them knew her name and who she was and some of them were her distant relatives. But at other times she felt uneasy, hearing only bits of the comments and remarks exchanged among them as they stood in their doorways or sat on their homemade chairs or overturned lobster crates. The remarks seemed mainly for themselves, to demonstrate their wit and masculinity to each other. As if they were young school boys instead of being mostly beyond middle age. Sometimes they reminded her of the late summer rams, playful and friendly and generally grazing contently in achadh nan caoraich, the field of sheep, although sometimes given to spontaneous rages against those who would trespass into their territory or sometimes unleashing their suppressed fury against one another.

"Are these lobsters from your dad's traps?"

"Yep."

"Where's he?"

"Out moving boats. You know there's a storm coming in?"

"No, I hadn't heard."

"We've got a bunch of boats coming in without much room. Nor'eastah. It's a full moon, too. The water will be higher than hell."

Suzanne passes me a lobster tail.

The first bite releases sea and wind and salt. It is a captured storm with the most appealing texture of anything that I've ever tasted—firm and crisp, brackish and satiating, and somehow reeking of promise, snapping between my teeth like seaweed bubbles.

"Do you need Dad for something?"

"Oh," I say, wiping the lobster juice from my lips, "I was just going to ask him about a boat. It can wait."

Max begins to cry. My interest in *Anne of Castine* seems to be the saddest thing in the world to him. His whining is reminiscent of a dog having been tethered too long, whining that is both desperate and hurt-sounding.

Suzanne bends over. "Maxxy." She pats his tiny head with the back of her juicy fingers. Max cries louder, which makes us both laugh, because his sounds have turned wordy and human-like, *Row, row, row, row.*

I wonder if he—like a dog bellowing before a devastating storm—is trying to alert us to something. *Row, row, row.* Crashing sounds come from the attic above. I picture the piled boxes tumbling from their high formation—life's sticky remnants—and then I recall the blue tarp, wondering if what lay beneath has finally awoken, some ghost with a tragic tale.

Suzanne doesn't appear concerned. She has grown accustomed to the moods of the building, which often cracks and teeters in the wind, just as she has grown accustomed to the moods of her father.

"Probably old paint cans," Suzanne says, even though I had pictured a woman, rising up from under the blue tarp and running . . .

. . . run . . . run . . . run.

The sun is now hidden, splattered over with gray clouds that tumble on the salty winds. Leaning on the doorframe, I recall a favorite painting of a large woman filling up the doorway of a fisherman's shanty. Her hair is wild—black as engine grease—and she is big, with hefty hands holding a bouquet of daisies. Her dress is ochre, darker than the seeds of the daisies, and there is a seagull perched on the saggy shanty roof. The woman doesn't appear to be waiting for anyone. It seems that she has picked the flowers for herself and that the day belongs to her. She doesn't even care if people believe she exists, and therefore has no need to play *He Loves Me, He Loves Me Not.*

Wind gusts whip my hair back and fondle my shirt. Imagining the cross within me, I try to stand straight like the lady in the shanty doorway. Surely, my dreams are not yet cinders. Surely, my original wish for myself still exists, even if I can't recall what it is.

Suzanne squeezes past with the pail of lobster carcasses.

"It's beautiful out there," I say.

"Yeah, but it's only teasing."

Max and I follow Suzanne to the edge of the deck. She empties the pail into the rising tide. The broken shells drop and then form a circle, floating in the sea foam like a sunburnt brood of children in a bubble bath.

A sharp pain cuts through the center of my forehead. The air pressure is low, which may be igniting a migraine. One often drops by in the afternoon, unrepentantly and with the gall of a crow. Each headache reminds me of my first, always arriving with the image of damnation. If the onset of my headaches has a sound, it would be that of an ax hitting wood. *Split.* After, the image of a dark cloud comes my way and when it recedes, I imagine my forehead having the texture of set clay. When I saw the skewed face of the Indian girl on the reservation so long ago, the girl chased by fire in her mother's womb, I thought at first she must be suffering from a horrible migraine.

Some of my migraines have been memorialized with the taste of injustice, the flavor of bitter rhubarb, my throat constricting, my jaw stiffening: a dead pony, a shot brother, the disappearance of a beloved dog, a favorite aunt trapped behind the bars of an asylum window, two friends killed in a car crash, and then the excruciating ache when each of my parents died. Each time, I rubbed my forehead raw. No amount of scrubbing would redeem me from the pain.

"Are you okay?" Suzanne asks, perhaps noticing my jaw beginning to stiffen or the lack of focus in my eyes.

"I'm getting a migraine."

A bright light flashes above her and then a series of dark rings break from it—auras—as solid-looking as rod iron. They are my pain's chain-link fence.

Rising above with X-ray vision, I would see myself trapped within that fence, my forehead imprinted with the image of lost paradise like fossils on a rock.

Rushing back to the sail loft, I know my jaw will relax minutes after I swallow the painkillers. I know I will put some music on and my mind will begin to float as the drug releases me from the circling black gate, and then rescues me from my prison of losses. My pharmaceutical redemption. Not a prescription that allows me to forget, but one that allows me to remember, my heartache momentarily buoyed and freed by a chemical, my fingers pressing across my once-throbbing forehead as if I am learning to read Braille.

Later, I remove the glass buoy from the net that Kenny gave to me, retrieving the green cracked blastula, smooth and pockmarked and as cool-feeling as morning dew on a porthole window. The fractured pattern reminds me of the tiny jellyfish that my daughters like to catch in jelly jars. Floating beneath the town dock at high tide, the embryos are a bouquet of embroidered cells. Holding them in a water-filled jar to the sun, the girls see everything that is necessary to form life. They see the living lace of blastulation.

Tucked at the bottom of the net in a dried piece of sugar kelp is a perfectly preserved skeleton of a shorthorn sculpin. No more than two inches long, and an exact replica of the ones that Jinx likes to chase and then devour. Carefully I lay it on the desk, next to the coral shaped like a man's hand and the rock shaped like a sideways heart.

three

*B*y chance, I am listening to old-time hymns sung by Anonymous 4—"Sweet Hour of Prayer," "Shall We Gather at the River," "Wondrous Love," "Sweet By and By"—all songs that I learned as a child in churches where people were not ashamed to fall on their knees or stand and give tear-filled testimonies of redemption, after praying the sinner's prayer.

I drove with Mom to Sunday-night services in evening summer light that stretched across the fields and stroked the freshly cut hayfields yellow. The breeze coming through the open windows was like countless hands stroking my face, the air fresh and satisfying with the sweet smell of mowed hay, my stomach rising and falling as we cruised up and down the hills toward the Maple Ridge church. Sometimes our car was full of worshippers whom Mom had invited to join us. She always went to prayer meeting and church expecting a miracle.

I often wondered what miracle she was expecting. What did she envision? Was it the miracle of salvation, was she expecting lost souls to come forward during the altar call, for me to finally get saved the right way, or was she expecting my Dean Martin father with his loosely held cigarette and bender tendencies to make a commitment soon, to come home? After all, she admitted to praying for him, and once I'd heard her tell him that he wasn't given nine lives for nothing.

"I wasn't?" Dad teased, no doubt cataloging some of his survival stories to himself: his car being T-boned by an oncoming train, a startled ardent moose cornering him deep in the woods that he was cruising, a log-skidder on which he was hitching a ride back across a frozen lake breaking through the ice, his repeated battles with cancer, its penetrating antlers coming at him again and again.

Or was Mom envisioning the ultimate miracle? Christ returning. Might he come back while we sat in the little wooden church, and if he did, what about Dad, who was home in his La-Z-Boy reading the newspaper and watching first the news and then Red Skelton, still uncommitted, never having prayed the sinner's prayer. What would happen to him? That glorious man who exuded comedic timing and gave unconditional love as easily as he breathed, that man who would someday plant a tree in honor of a dead pony. Would he get to go, too? Would there be enough warning for the so-called sinners to still repent—an alerting uneasy rustling before the trumpets—or would he be left behind while the TV laugh track ran on like a bubbling brook, and Red Skelton signed off with his lisping, predictable, yet sincere *God Bless.*

And what about my brothers who we'd left playing baseball in the field with our cousins? Would they be raptured? I'd heard one swearing geehovahje-sus when he'd struck out earlier, so would he be left behind while others rose to the heavens? We'd all heard that tattered verse—*One will be taken while the other will be left behind*—favored by the churches that we attended. We'd all felt the threatening cold chill of it trickle down the backs of our necks.

Years later, when Dad finally embraced the teachings of Christ, he would still panic if he woke and found Mom missing from their bed. He'd tell her when he finally found her soaking away her arthritis in the bath or at her desk writing to one of her grown children, that he thought maybe she'd been rap-tured and he'd been left behind, his newfound faith somehow unworthy. Mom said he always said this playfully, his gold-crowned tooth beaming from the corner of his half-grin. Still, I suspect it was one of his deepest fears, especially as he grew older. His *afraid.* Just as it was mine. To be left behind. To not be raptured. And I suspect Dad, like my siblings and I, felt that it was Mom that tethered us to the Divine, her kneeling prayers and petitions keeping our heavenly path open, no matter how far we strayed or what swearing words came from our lips. She would faithfully nurture the parterre.

From a young age, I felt her prayers surrounding me, the bubble of them sometimes visible, a clear and polished glow, which matched the glow of her face.

As a child and then young adult, I was fearless in discovering the world. Any number of situations could have left me damaged in one way or another, but I had been miraculously protected from many things: hitchhiking, an aggressive Italian boy, a stint attending after-hours modeling parties where bowls of cocaine were displayed like candy, traveling great distances at night and alone, sailing in storms, a casting director who flashed me during an audition, a car crash, rheumatic fever at the age of twenty-two, and a sassy mouth with a mindless tendency to defend others. One winter night, while walking on a Toronto sidewalk with my Antiguan friend, a stranger passed and spit on her. I grabbed the perpetrator's hood, trying to turn him back to me so I could scold him, but all he returned was his fist so hard against my temple that I fell backwards and then blacked out, waking with an injustice headache like no other. Above me, the glow of streetlights bloated like splatters of white paint and my friend's voice saying my name sounded as if she was at the end of a tunnel.

Coming home from the risky world, I took the path that Mom had left open, that parterre blessed with her bespoke prayers, a trail that led to the garden room of her, my earth mother, my Godly one. Pressing my face to her cheek, I smelled lavender and hay and the world fell away. The sweet seeds of her scent broke like a healing salve upon my lips. And I felt forgiven in her presence, her consecrated existence pardoning me better than any painkiller.

————

The sound of Ottmar Liebert's Spanish guitar induces emotions as soothing as gentle waves—whispering and washing over fields of sand—receding, disappearing, only to return—whispering, washing, receding, disappearing, the ocean without wilderness.

Henry Beston said there is beauty in the sound of a wave, but also ancient terror. Sometimes late at night when the harbor is quiet, I sit on the sail loft deck, breathing in the salty timber rot, and listening to the waves out beyond the bell buoy. The slight echoing hint of thunder in the bell reminds me of a recurring dream of paddling the Bahamian seas in a wooden canoe. The water is turquoise and shallow and I have the feeling of serenity, but suddenly I am over deeper, darker water and the waves are beginning to rock the canoe. First gently and then more threateningly. Instantly, I know that I have accidentally reached the edge of the continental shelf. The water is no longer shallow, but black and fathomless. Clearly, I am up against a force that has its own elemental laws and I am nothing to it. In the dream, I keep thinking only my mother's fervent prayers could save me.

Since the sea has always brought me peace, then why is it also part of my subconscious terror? And is this terror ancient or is it pending? Could it be autobiography as nightmare? Might an ancestor of mine have floated on an open sea waiting to be rescued? And might the dream of falling from the sail loft into the water be connected to the dream of canoeing over the continental shelf? Or could the dreams stem from Mom's tales of Poseidon—the turbulent God of the seas—or maybe the dreams are to remind me of her teaching that no one with faith remains hopeless, for in these dreams, the canoe does not completely tip over, nor do I drown while being thrashed in the waves. I simply search frantically for an air bubble before waking.

Liebert's music is without terror, though. It is lying on a warm beach, oiled and unconcerned, it is listening to my daughters as they chase the screeching terns, while their father skips a flat stone across the water. Once, a stone he threw at the backshore beach skipped a reversed Fibonacci pattern and after the first dozen or so bounces, the last few were so indistinguishably close that the stone appeared to be walking on water.

Barrett Martin's *Painted Desert* liner notes say, *My music is the result of being thirsty and going to the desert, thirsty for truth and meaning in a world that seems to be fast forgetting both.* Barrett's drumming resurrects the memory of Pony's thumping canter, wild and daring, steady and trustworthy, ancient but without terror. *Watch, listen, and remember, because as children of the Creator, we are all worthy of this knowledge.*

"Black Is the Color of My True Love's Hair" by Nina Simone was a gift from Bill. He saw her perform at the Montreux Jazz Festival years ago, and said that before her performance she lectured the audience, confessing she had just watched a documentary on Janis Joplin, saying how Janis was pouring her heart out on stage to "an audience of corpses." Bill mimicked Simone's imperious English inflection, and the statement had become a useful code between us, whenever we needed to alert the other to a pending tedious situation. An audience of corpses.

Nina's glassy voice often sings with longing for a kind of love that can only exist in one's past, a love gone by, the kind that harbors a desire to someday return no matter how dangerous it may be. The continental shelf of love. The one best left to memories and dreams. While canoeing in the shallow water of contemplation, one languishes as if unaware of danger, as if floating beneath a healing tree. *Willow, willow, bend for me.*

Simone reminds me of the letter that I sent after my mother's death, on the day that I was to meet him for lunch: *Mom died yesterday at two in the afternoon. It was a halcyon day, a flock of white butterflies escorted her away from us and onto that heaven-bound train. I have the feeling that she departed to keep me from seeing you, so best you not contact me again.*

For years before my marriage, we were constantly reuniting. An architect that knew all the trees of the world and probably just as many women, and an expert at manipulating both, the wood to a shiny gloss, the women to a pliable presence. Still, my husband was the only one to rival him for my affection. After marrying, I simply sent a postcard from Europe. *Married now.*

Even then I had the good sense to know that one who loves many, loves none. It seemed ridiculous that I had now allowed myself to be charmed by a letter with a series of reminiscences, that I had let my fascination with my youth buoy me like the salty sea, while it surreptitiously soaked and weakened my timbers. Why?

four

With the consistent wave of pain medication, my tightly held jaw finally gives way like a prison gate collapsing. Then I begin to catalog what I am reading, a self-imposed exercise to convince me that the use of painkillers will not keep me from thinking clearly.

Dog on the Cross by Aaron Gwyn is an exquisite collection of stories—a careful articulation of faith and doubt, sin and self-delusion, allegiance to the church and self-glorification—but more so, they are stories like old hymns that remind me of my early spiritual witnessing. Wednesday-night prayer meetings with Mom as we kneeled at creaky wooden benches to pray with others, or as one of the old-timers in that church often said, to partition Jesus. Now I know the word is *petition*, but as a child, I had unknowingly looked *partition* up in the dictionary: to separate or divide, which was a disturbing meaning. It was certainly not the feeling I had on the swing that day. Rather, I felt as if I was part of something grand.

Partition seems more fitting to the feeling that I have now, to the tired feeling of being pried apart by two forces. An admired apologist recently suggested this weary feeling doesn't come from what we don't have, but from what we have. Instantly, I'd felt the weight of my houses and cars, my trips planned and unplanned, my faithful Day-Timer that records my cleaning help and yard help and child help, checkups and tune-ups, beauty appointments, my heavy-laden closets, my jewelry and makeup and potions, and the many other belongings that I've collected over the years, both large and small. I imagined all these things piled between me and the simple things that had shaped me as a child, all so sweet then. Even then, I knew sacred. The shedding of light, the encompassing of prayer, hope and peace uniquely united. Wonder. Nothing now spiritually compares to kneeling with Mom or praying on the swing. To think that as a little girl in a small church with worn benches and the air smelling like the inside of a cedar box, I knelt to petition a supreme being, as houseflies buzzed against the closed windows, frantically trying to escape.

Why was this all flooding back?

Was it Anonymous 4 singing the hymn Mom often sang, "In the Sweet By and By," or was it the wood-smelling sail loft reminding me of the little church, or was it that Mom had been dead for a year now, and each day, I missed her more, felt myself seeping into the hole of her death, until I simply seemed a cutout, which remained.

Was it that I'd recently watched *The Passion of the Christ*, the rendition of evil so hauntingly portrayed that the image wakes me at night, twisting around my bedposts like the worm in Lucifer's mouth. Waking, I have the same terror as waking from that recurring dream of floating over the continental shelf. Lying in my bed, I know that kind of evil exists, and then I wonder if my busy life has kept me from being aware of it. Watching the movie, I'd concluded that I had never doubted the story of Christ. Throughout my life, it had remained real, but somehow as an adult, I had managed to soft-pedal the story of evil, treating its horrific images as nightmares, better off forgotten. So I was a believer without having contemplated evil. At least, not since listening to the fire-and-brimstone sermons of my youth. *One shall be taken, while another one left behind.*

I knew evil existed—had even toyed with it myself. I saw evil reported every day in the guise of war and rape and murder, but I had chosen to picture it as a kind of hazy fog that floated somewhere in the distance. Hadn't I battened down the hatches by choosing a kind and faithful husband, and then a small quaint village to raise our children, a place tucked away from the truly dangerous sins of this world?

Suddenly, Satan as a Super Being, as a deity, one capable of being equally present—or even more present—than Christ in my life was a concern. This coupled with the absence of my prayer-warrior mother often reduced me to desperation. Sometimes I fell on the sail loft floor and cried the same way I cried over my parents' grave. Once, I fell asleep on the floor and dreamed that I was looking into a mirror, staring at my pried-open self. There, I saw a withered heart. When touched, it was as small and hard as the heart-shaped stone that I'd brought back from Grays Island. And when I woke, there the stone lay on the desk, next to the coral shaped like a man's waving hand.

I longed for Mom. I missed her the way I missed the presence of my newborns when I wasn't holding them. Something of her eternalness had stayed, a sweet vagueness like perfume after a party, but her body was gone, the shape of it extracted from me like a crucial and necessary organ, the raw opening whispering, Who are you without her?

And who was asking?

And where was she?

Where was my mother?

In heaven? A place where we will be rewarded with streets of gold after the many Christian teachings that say we shouldn't care about possessions?

WHERE WAS MY MOTHER?

Surely not in the lonely cemetery.

Once while comforting me at Dad's graveside, she said, "Sweetheart, there is nothing as lonely as a loved one's grave."

"Why?" I asked.

Mom looked at the line of tombstones beyond, all belonging to grandparents and uncles and aunts and cousins that had gone before Dad.

"Because they are not here," she said, "and somehow knowing that they are with Christ isn't enough. Our minds are too small."

To me, that was Mom at her spiritual best, the place where her religion was unable to fill in all the gaps, and she was admitting it. And certainly my flimsy beliefs had not taken care of me when she died. Where was Mom, and what had happened to her on that departing day?

Over the past year, I'd searched out facts, approaching her death like a research project, trying to avoid spiraling down. Studies done by a Dutch cardiologist with patients who had near-death experiences revealed that after Mom pushed her quilt back and called, *Evangeline, I'm ready*, she rose above her earthly body to enter a tunnel of warm white light that was devoid of fear and pain. With that first step, the research said her entire life passed before her. In the past, these experiences were attributed to physiological, psychological, pharmacological, or religious reasons, but Dr. van Lommel's studies reveal our brains are not capable of storing everything we experience in our lifetime. They are too small. The study concluded that near-death experiences can only be explained if we assume that consciousness, along with all our experiences and memories, is located somewhere else, outside our bodies. Van Lommel suspects there is a dimension where information is stored, a kind of collective consciousness we tune into to gain access to our identity and memories. He believes we tune into consciousness through our DNA, that our DNA works like a receptor mechanism to attune us to our memories and consciousness, and even to the memories of our blood relatives. Reading this, I couldn't help but wonder if that was why Italians became so ill viewing those Renaissance paintings, helplessly attuned to their ancestors' pain through their DNA—autobiography as nightmare.

The idea that my parents might still be connected to me through our shared DNA comforted me. I believed that they were with Christ, that they had entered into the permanent shedding of light, but still I wondered if I'd be protected from the kind of evil portrayed in the Passion without my mother's prayers.

Who are you without her?

Whose voice was asking? Was it the chant of the Cannered Noz? Was I about to die without absolution? Were the washerwomen preparing to scrub linens on my behalf? Or was I destined for damnation—that dark image that accompanied my first migraine headache—that feeling of being overcome by a great black cloud, and then something sharp hitting my forehead: *Split*. A split that partitioned Mom from me, a split that came from a feeling of being judged.

five

*T*he back door swings open and the wind escorts my family into the sail loft as if they are being pushed by a crowd, the wind rejoicing, gloating and teasing us with its feathery lips. Phoebe leads carrying a pizza and Georgia is right behind, smiling, a book as always tucked beneath her arm. All summer she has been reading about ghosts. Yesterday, she told me that if I was ever bothered by one to firmly say, Go away.

Bill is behind them, carrying the mail, which I have not bothered to pick up since he left for California.

"You're home," I applaud.

His handsome good looks surprise me. Not because I forget he is good-looking, just that I forget how good-looking he really is. Closing my eyes, I can flip through a series of images of him coming through a series of back doors, starting when we were first married and living in those servants' quarters on the South Shore of Boston. He was twenty-six, his hair as shiny as coal. Twenty years of a man returning, twenty years of a man coming through a back door. The thought is as comforting as the smell of chamomile is soothing.

"Pizza, Mama, pizza." Phoebe rushes to the sofa, holding the large box up and smiling, her square baby teeth a heavenly bluish-white.

I take the warm box, putting it on the low table in front of us. The smell of yeasty dough and tomato and melted cheese wafts between us like a muggy cloud. She crawls onto my lap and I kiss her face that smells salty and balmy from the wind. Her body is cool pudding, her skin as smooth and alluring as the sensuous words that inspired her.

Georgia plops down beside us, hugging my neck and vying for equal time. She, too, smells of dough and of the wind and of a honeyed nectar that embodies girls. I think how each of them was once a wind that blew in each of us and how our blended winds created them. What better restitution.

Bill drops the mail on the table, and then leans over and kisses my mouth with lips that are thick and hefty and determined. He looks into my eyes. "How are you?"

"Good."

"How are your headaches?"

"Constant. My neck is stiff. How was California?"

"Sad."

I see the flash of *afraid* in his eyes and touch his face, which is tanned. He winks and pulls away. Yesterday on the telephone, he said he couldn't get the sight of the little white casket out of his mind. *It hit me like a wall.*

I pull Phoebe to my chest. She snuggles for just a moment, and then pulls away, wiggling down by my side. She sucks on two fingers, watching the boisterous bay. She points to the masts of three rocking boats.

"Look, Mama," she says, "crosses. Jesus," she says, sitting up and tugging on my shirt as if trying to alert me to something very important.

"Yes, sweetie." I smile, and she smiles, too, her faith in images as pure as her flawless skin.

Cleaning her closet not long ago, I found a pile of dusty white sand. When I asked her what is was, she said that it was the body of Christ.

"Where did you get it?" I asked.

"At communion," she said. "I hide the wafers in my pocket."

"Do you play with the wafers? Is that why they have turned to dust?"

"Oh yes," she said, beaming. "I play with them all the time."

I sat on her bed as she continued to line her plastic farm animals across her bedroom floor. There were calves and lambs and piglets and they were following a large cow wearing a Barbie crown. Phoebe talked to the animals as if they were human, telling them that the royal cow was taking them to a big field. She told them it was full of clover. It will be heaven. I thought of the communion dust, white and powdery, and how she as a child knew that she was not only to meet Christ at church, but she was to bring Him home as a playmate. It didn't matter if she rubbed him until he turned to dust. He was still with her, as trustworthy as a guiding royal cow.

"Daddy," Phoebe says. He is standing beside us watching the sea as if in a trance. "Daddy." She leans forward and pulls on his jeans. "Sit with us. Sit." She pats his place on the sofa.

We align ourselves, facing the dark blue ruffled sea and watch as the *Isabelle* hauls *Caution* past the sail loft and upriver. Georgia leans over and picks up Max, who has been faithfully standing by. She rubs noses with him, letting him lick her lips, and we all snuggle down. The wind has become more humid, begging the salty sweet from the girls' faces, mixing it with their father's spices, a brew of calming vapor, a soothing tea that seeps and then expands. Family.

I cross one leg over Bill. He leans up and looks at my calf, rubbing lightly near the swollen red gouge. "How did you get this cut?"

"I fell through the broken step behind the boatyard and a nail caught me."

"Kenny needs to fix that."

"Kenny needs to fix a lot of things."

"How did you fall?"

"Going home in the dark. I forgot about it."

"You'd better get it checked." He looks for streaks up my leg. "Really, it looks infected. When was your last tetanus shot?"

"It's fine. I've been soaking it in the sea."

"The sea doesn't cure everything."

"It doesn't?"

The white-capped bay has turned wilder and the water is now as high as hell, just like Suzanne promised. Swelling in a way that suggests it may not be able to contain itself. It could spill over like a foaming experiment gone wrong. Only the three boats are left on their moorings, the others having been hauled away or moved on up the river into coves, and they are beginning to rock frantically. I imagine them coming loose and racing out to sea. If the storm is nasty enough, the whole shore could wash away, sail lofts and boathouses and docks, all of them leaving as if to rush willingly toward a long-awaited promise.

Beyond the islands and Brooksville, the sky has turned as gray as goose down, with edges that seep the stony color of a deep quarry. Infant winds squeeze through the slightly open slider door, free of their busy parents, whipping through the sail loft, warm and brackish, and caressing our faces.

"It's tropical," Bill says.

"Like the Bahamas."

We recall that as newlyweds we boated to a Bahamian island renowned for its conch shells, each exhibiting a pink so beautiful that the color should have a different name, something that might suggest girls and music and dancing. *Pinkala.* Near the island, we came across an abandoned Cigarette boat, floating in a cove beneath the brutal sun. It had been painted steely gray and its shape resembled a barracuda. Still, it might as well have been a coffin, for that was the feeling it emitted. I asked Bill to steer closer, to let me look inside, but he said it was a drug-running boat and we were staying away. It was the first time that he resisted me firmly. I, on the other hand, felt the boat might tell a story, one that I could easily claim. I argued that maybe there were dead bodies in the boat, maybe we should call the Coast Guard, but he shook his head, no. As we motored on, I sulked. Later he said, You shouldn't go looking for trouble, Deborah. Looking for trouble? I wondered then if that was the same as Mom's warning for me not to take unnecessary chances.

The girls tell us they painted rocks with their babysitter, Heather, and then sold them to the tourists who passed in front of our house.

"One man bought two," Georgia says, pulling away, breaking the bread of us first. She puts Max down and then picks up the pizza box and takes it to the long table. "I'm sad because I sold my favorite scene."

"What was it?" I ask.

"It was one of all of us at the backshore, skipping stones."

I don't blame her for wanting to keep it. She is growing up and no doubt sees the bridge to becoming a young woman before her. Her journey thus far gathering like sediment in the bottom of her heart, like sand blown into a pinkala shell. The dregs of this family tea have stained the porcelain of her, and she, like most daughters, will find it hard to leave. She like me will no doubt spend her life being pulled back home.

Phoebe follows Georgia and Max follows Phoebe, excited with the prospect of a crumb being dropped or a crust being offered. When given a crust, he will take it to a corner and savor it like a bone. He will worship it until it is nothing but dust.

"There's lemonade in the fridge," I say, resisting the urge to set them up with plates and napkins and silverware. After all, I am trying to let go of domesticity here. Even so, I have found few joys as great as feeding my children. From the beginning, they opened their mouths as trustfully as baby birds. Looking at the blossom of their lips, it was hard not to view it as a calling.

Outside, the day has lost several degrees of light and the dark quarry borders are beginning to seep and blot the whole sky. Bill and I hug one another and he plays with the fringes on my cutoffs, and then rubs my bottom, tapping a tune with his fingers as if to keep rhythm with the wind not outside, but within him. Ever the drummer and cymbal maker, he is always tapping: my thigh, his thigh, a table, the top of our daughters' heads, a steering wheel, a railing.

He kisses my forehead that is sore from aching. His familiar lips ease it. I breathe in his cinnamon and cardamom and mint, rubbing my hand up and down the back of his starched shirt and along his spine, picturing it as a great and powerful zipper. Behind it is a commanding heart, its grip on me light, but as strong as a matador's if the need be. As always our familiarity entices the erotic. It is an undertow mirrored by our sandy hearts and teasing winds. To resist its pull, Bill slaps my bottom, sits up, and then begins going through the stack of mail.

Tossing me a letter, he smiles, winks, and then whispers *Boyfriend*, as if alerting me to a gnawing presence, not a threatening one, but similar to Max chewing on a crust. I frown, *Mmm*, looking at the stamp and date, June 6, the first anniversary of Mom's death. He waited a year. I slip it behind a sofa cushion, and then tuck it with the dust deep in the sofa's seams. My heart has sped up, but I try to act otherwise, massaging Bill's neck and asking if he is tired. He says he had a nap on the plane.

I ask him what he would like for dinner.

"I had a late lunch and the kids have had their pizza so I may skip dinner. How 'bout you?"

"If you're not eating, I'll have something here."

"Good, babe. I'll take you out tomorrow night."

"It's a date. I may work late tonight."

He squeezes my thigh, and then moves away.

I wonder, as I have before, why the shadow of another man doesn't seem to concern him. If anything it seems to free him, as if he would be happy to share me, to have another absorbing my usual thoughts and worries that even unmentioned can sometimes weigh on him. Perhaps it is because he has his own worries.

He picks up a *New Yorker* and heads for a wicker chair, sitting and flipping through its pages. He looks tired, and even tomorrow after he gets a good night's sleep, a dusting of that tired look will remain, not yet a stain, but soon to be, as he has been sensing something amiss in his family's business, a younger brother's tireless ambition to push him out. Why? Because in a family led by a narcissist, there are constant games designed to test one's allegiance to the leader. Winning often means being unethical, which my husband is not.

I sense it is a bludgeoning coming his way that may leave a hole I won't be able to fill. A black well. It is more than I can bring myself to think about, and perhaps that is why Bill pays so little attention to an old lover's letter; perhaps the possibility of my betrayal is more than he can contemplate just now.

One should rather die than be betrayed. There is no deceit in death. It delivers precisely what it has promised. Betrayal, though . . . betrayal is the willful slaughter of hope.

———

My family leaves—rushing out when the heavy slanted rains appeared across the bay—coming down in dark sheets. Watching them hurry toward the darkening parking lot and then turning up the hill with Max held firmly in Georgia's arms, I imagine the girls grown, and the years to come, and what it will mean when they take on lives of their own, fading from the vision of a father with two young daughters. I can't imagine it meaning anything but loneliness. The nest void of blossoming mouths, a mother's sustenance no longer necessary, my memories of them heavier than my unmentioned worries could ever be. Who will comfort me if not my husband? Who will comfort him, if not me? And who will model family for our girls now, if not us?

The town dock and the parked cars turn blurry with rain and wind. The pounding on the roof is like handfuls of sand being thrown by an army. Kenny's red truck races away and the other boatyard men drive out in their battered trucks behind him. Barring an emergency, the workers will not return until morning, but Kenny comes and goes so often during stormy nights that he appears as a ghost. A few nights ago while walking home through the boatyard, I thought I glimpsed his shadow, but saw no further evidence of him. It was as if I had firmly said, *Go away.*

I crack the front slider door wider, letting a brood of child winds in, whisking the smell of pizza away, because to retrieve the letter with the scent of my children's sustenance still present feels predatory. The sail loft seems to sway in the wind, and for the shortest second I picture it floating away with me in it, the image somehow reassuring rather than threatening.

I walk around the room, switching on lamps, touching the long table and then the chairs. I look at the boy's portrait and the cow's skull and then study the picture of the sail loft man. His gaze no longer appears distant, but intent and concentrated, and like the eyes cast on the Shroud of Turin, they also appear sad.

The *Wages of Sin* posters hang over the single bed. The owners of the sail loft said that sea captains brought the posters back to a local woman. Maybe she was a restless woman, too, or maybe in love with one of the sea captains, or two or three. Researching the play, *The Wages of Sin*, I found a *New York Times* review written on May 13, 1884. "The play's author takes the ground, evidently, that women in love are like soldiers in battle—blind to danger . . ."

The review reminded me of a remark by the poet Anne Carson. "When an ecstatic is asked the question, What is it that love dares the self to do? She will answer: Love dares the self to leave itself behind, to enter into poverty."

———

The cream-colored envelope is thick and stiff. There is an embossed eagle where the return address should be. The penmanship is heavy and loopy, reminding me of the black circles that come from the auras of a migraine. From my books on handwriting, I have learned that his holds some warning signs: a heavy hand; control. Not good for a woman used to a husband that sets few limits. The lower case of the *f* letter looping backwards: a versatile sex life. Not good for a woman whose heart races when his letter arrives. Vertical writing that could suggest diplomacy, but also indifference. Not good if he somehow manages to seduce me, and then grows weary of a woman who betrayed her own family.

What poverty.

While the rains beats down, I open the Franklin stove. Its hinges whine with rust. I dip my finger into the cool and silken ashes beneath the grate, and then draw a black cross on the envelope, recalling his enticing stories: a boy during the war, an occupied village, American soldiers giving him chocolate, the body of a suicide victim hanging in a barn, a teenage illness, an aloof father, a strict and indiscreet mother, a champion skier, a collector of wood, of famous clients, of cars, of homes, of women. *All in my past and holy.*

Why go back?

The tug started with his memories of me. Me. While searching for my youth in his reflective pond, I missed intuiting Mom's death. While obsessing on my past, the present had been muted. I allowed myself to float aimlessly on a vaporous sea, imagining a man's strong hand reaching down to rescue me from my day-to-day. Me. Afraid to let go of my youth.

Looking up the word *infidelity* shortly after Mom died, I found the definition beginning with *To break a promise*, and was unable to continue reading.

———

Even though I feel feverish and hot, I stuff bunched newspapers along with kindling into the stove. The warm night wind howls down the flue, creating a storm bowl of ashes that smells both oily and lovely. Breathing deeply, I imagine some fraction of the breath of my redeemer hidden like a golden coin in the cinders. *Help me.*

Save me.

When I light the newspaper, the flames curl, the kindling snaps, the blaze extinguishing yesterday's print. How compelling the headlines were. Now, they seem so trite. No different than a flirtation. That is what Mom felt that day in the old-age home, *regret*, and that is what I feel now.

Closing my eyes and leaning in, I hold my face as close to the fire for as long as I possibly can, which is no more than a few seconds. *You could have been born a girl with a melted-looking face, but your mother took care of you even when you were in her womb. Yes, you were loved. You are loved.*

I drop the letter on the fire without opening it and the cindery cross begins to disappear. The creamy envelope rolls back like a scroll and the black and heavy handwriting with its heavy letters melt. I'd like to say its contents begin to feel as trite as yesterday's news, but that would be a lie. Colorful flames lick and then open the letter, revealing a photograph of me, young and smiling, wearing my father's fedora, my eyes inviting. I watch the hat burn like straw, my face burn like cloth, the fire hissing and then dying down quickly. My regret pulses harder as if I have just sold one of my favorite painted scenes to a tourist.

When I poke the smoldering letter with a stick, there are remnants of my face, half-burnt. For a moment, I want to retrieve the pieces so that I can glue them back together. A portrait of me when I was young. How silly. Like Mom, I now know that I had spent too many hours contemplating an unresolved love, and in doing so, I had lost precious time.

————

Curling like a question mark on the sofa, I'm tempted to take another pain pill, but I would be taking it more for the feeling of unsettlement than for pain, even though my neck seems to be getting stiffer and hurting more. I know that making painkillers a companion is dangerous, no different than the constant companionship of booze or a careless friend or an ongoing flirtation, and I know that I am already teaching my body to surrender to it as if surrendering to a saving nap. Despite the lulling feeling it delivers, it is a beast. Someday, it could reel and lasso me, a desire so lacking in logic that my eyes will glean folly from the promise it has trapped me in. And what does it promise me? A painless visit to my youth, my loves and losses, my heart dulled just enough for my mind to travel back.

Unsettlement, I say aloud. *Unsettlement.* That's it. It crackles like a fire and holds its heat like a pile of coals. It smolders in my chest. It leaves a residue that can rot. That is the noun of my being. It is the thing that Mom recognized as a tendency for taking unnecessary chances and my husband recognizes as looking for trouble. It is neither fluid nor pretty. A word of explanation. *Unsettlement.* A word that one might see stamped on a cold-case file. I have harbored the word of myself forever. I see it in my own handwriting, the lower zone of my *y*'s often becoming elongated and suggesting restlessness. A restlessness born with my first migraine, a splitting of myself in two. My two selves.

I look at my palm lines, rubbing the remaining ash over the longest ones that are Mom and Dad, and then over the triangle like a sail that is Bill and Georgia and Phoebe. I touch my siblings and nieces and nephews and aunts and uncles and cousins and friends, my childhood home, my pets, Duchess and Pony and Sailor, the wooden churches, the swimming hole, my favorite beaches, and all the X-shaped marks for all the songs of birds that I once knew, and then like a whisper it arrives, the murmur that I felt content and settled when I recognized all the songs of birds, their chorus chanting, *Know me.*

(And I did.)

I rush to look for Jinx, but it is now dark and impossible to see anything on the water. It has stopped raining, but the halyards are still clanging in the winds. There is no bird calling, nothing of Jinx's staccato stuttering. How I long to see his spread wings. Earlier, after my family left, an unfamiliar sail-boat with two sailors landed on Jinx's favorite mooring ball that belongs to *Caution.* One sailor shooed Jinx away with a boat hook. I screamed at the sailor. The wind simply carried my words away like tumbleweed on a prairie. *Stop. Do not touch him.*

Neither man looked my way.

They had sailed toward the mooring in a large and battered wooden yawl with the middle sail flapping and snapping. Motoring in might have been better, since the high winds had already arrived and the waves were thrashing, but they seemed to need to show off their handling ability. I've often noticed that strangers who sail in almost always motor out. And I wondered then how quickly they would tire of Castine, how soon another destination would beckon them. Like other visitors, they would no doubt take what they wanted and be gone by sunrise. A harbor is a harbor is a harbor.

Still, the sailors claimed the harbor as if it belonged to them. Near the mooring, their boat rocked recklessly, yet Jinx tried to hold his own, his black wings spread in defiance. Sitting in profile, his crooked neck was exaggerated and his chest propelled forward in the way of a determined warrior, yet he also appeared desperate, as if he might be suffocating, his neck bobbing in and out, his orange gullet appearing swollen. He took a swipe from the heavyset sailor before lifting off, flying low over the turbulent waters toward the islands. I'd never seen him so close to a human, and for the shortest second, a pang of jealousy spread through me, and then a second, more cutting, pang. *Injustice*, I wanted to yell. The moment conjured my losses: a cat, a dog, a pony, my father, my mother, my, my . . .

Maybe Jinx needed the mooring left free so he could continue drying his wings, or had he simply wanted those men to leave? Maybe he despised their showing off, or his defiance might have come from a greater knowledge, some collective consciousness that wildlife can access through their DNA. Long ago, his ancestors, the spectacled cormorants, now extinct, were killed and eaten by shipwrecked sailors in the Northern Pacific. Only one naturalist ever witnessed this bird, and in the end, he, too, was shipwrecked, and had eaten them as a matter of survival. Maybe Jinx was feeling the ancient truth of his sea crow lineage—*autobiography as nightmare.*

It was after Jinx disappeared that I noticed the smaller sailor wearing the lady's floppy straw hat that had blown out to sea earlier. I pictured him nabbing it with the boat hook, and then pinning it to the guardrail like an octopus to dry. The hat somehow suited him, as if he were a playful Puck, as if he had blown in on a nor'easter to be a trickster through the storm. From a distance, his agility was boy-like, nimble, but the curve of his shoulders suggested middle age.

Once on the mooring, he removed the straw hat, tossing it like a Frisbee belowdecks. Then, he wrapped the flapping sail in a matter of seconds and jumped into the rubber dinghy as if it were a trampoline. His heavyset partner joined him, weighing down the dinghy as it motored toward Kenny's dock, his face jutting forward, his shoulders hunkered around his chest as if it were a cave of stolen treasures, a pirate's trove. Again, I thought of Yeats, *The half-read wisdom of daemonic images, Suffice the ageing man as once the growing boy.*

Maybe Jinx flew off to find a lover, the white tufts on her head appearing as a wedding crown and beckoning him, or maybe he had been hurt by the boat hook. From a distance I could not tell if the hook had only come close or if it had touched his orange gullet, unnecessarily. The thought made my throat throb. I liken it to the makeshift hole in my uncle's throat after he had his larynx removed, maimed yet crimson and still pulsing. The thought echoed my losses, my . . . *afraid*. Somewhere beneath was my original wish for myself. Yes. It beat like a drum in a barrack and made me long for home.

> *Anytime you go back*
> *the familiar underpulse*
> *will start its throbbing: HOME, HOME!*
> *and the hole torn and patched over*
> *will gape unseen again.*

six

*L*ying on the sofa, I see the churches that I attended when I was young. The Baptist church on a nearby knoll, and the three Wesleyan Methodist churches that sat like satellites beyond the valley. Mom went where she was needed, always taking her children with her. She delivered sermons when a church was without a pastor, and recited countless object lessons while teaching Sunday school. She turned our family car that Dad kept polished and smelling of peppermint into a church taxi that she loaded up with kids who sometimes smelled sour and whose parents were often still sleeping off the booze from the night before. What noun lived in those parents? What was their imposing noun of self?

For a time, in a church abandoned by a wayward preacher, Mom took over as the full-time pastor, ordaining me at twelve as the pianist. I was a mediocre player at best, so I frantically designed my own play-by-number hymnal. Note numbers corresponding with finger numbers seemed much simpler than actually studying the music. In an old hymnal from home, I once found a written list of my lazily rehearsed play-by-number songs:

"What a Friend"
"Love Lifted Me"
"Stand Up for Jesus"
"This Is My Father's House"
"The Old Rugged Cross"
"Trust and Obey"
"In the Sweet By and By"
"It Is Well With My Soul"

Mom also put me in charge of wildflower arrangements for the offering table, and instructed me to teach Sunday school while she gave the sermon.

"I can't teach Sunday school," I said.

"Of course you can. Go ahead. Jump in." The very same words that she had first uttered to me at the swimming hole.

Aubrey, who was ten, was in charge of sweeping out the dead flies before church began, and of taking up the collection, which he was to count and seal in a white envelope at the end of the service.

Sitting at the little Sunday school table, the drunkards' children scratched their arms that were covered with mosquito bites. They looked at me with dazed expressions, caused, I suppose, by witnessing the noun of their parents over and over. It had left their faces lacking illumination like waning moons. From the beginning, I hated them. Loving them as my mother instructed—as God loves you—would have changed everything, creating all sorts of hope in them, and although I could not have put this into words then, I feared being responsible for that hope. I feared being stuck pretending to love them. Who knew what kind of love it might take to lift them from their bleak circumstances. Years later, I confessed this to Mom, and after looking at me for a moment, she said, "That's where God's love comes in. It's never waning. Never feeble."

The word *feeble* insulted me.

"What are you suggesting?" I asked.

"I'm suggesting that in those situations you simply attempt to be a conduit for God's love. It can't begin with you." Mom sounded perplexed as if this was Love 101, and something that I should have already known. "Without Him," she added, "our wells run dry."

———

The little church had three members: Mr. Arthur Stairs, a bald, limping man who cried when he prayed and cried when he gave his testimony or recited verses. *What wondrous love is this! Oh my soul! That caused the Lord of bliss to bear the dreadful curse for my soul, for my soul, To bear the dreadful curse for my soul.*

The other two members were Mr. and Mrs. Dodson, a dignified tall man with a repertoire of *Amens* and *Blessed Jesus* that he used to punctuate Mom's sermons. His hands and feet were immense, a trick often used by Renaissance sculptors to make their figures more evocative, as in Michelangelo's *David*. Mythic. When Mr. Dodson entered the church and held his dress hat in his hands, the hat looked comical and miniature, something for a doll, while he appeared larger than life, a balding Hercules.

Mrs. Dodson was shorter than Aubrey and stout, her neck hidden inside round, raised shoulders, her black-rimmed eyeglasses tight against small dark eyes and pudgy cheeks. She was always smiling and nodding as if to say *yes, yes, yes*, reminding me of a nodding dog that sometimes sat in the back window of a car. Once on the Trans-Canada Highway, we had traveled behind a car in which the nodding dog's head had come loose and rolled to the corner of the back window like a ball.

Together, the Dodsons were an odd yet somehow wonderfully matched couple. They had a married daughter and three teenage boys who sometimes attended church, but mostly stayed home to run the farm. Their home sat along a dirt road where traffic seldom passed, up beyond one of the hills that I watched from home, wondering if my real life existed somewhere beyond. It was to that farm we would eventually deliver our dog, Duchess.

A black collie—wet-eyed, with matted coat and crouching—she had arrived early one Saturday morning with Dad, returning from what we surmised had been an all-night poker game. No doubt she had been the last contribution to the poker pot. Our shed was full of useless things brought home from betting games, or to our door by hungover men who needed money quickly. Dad always accepted their offerings graciously, and then pulled out his billfold. Once he told me while organizing the multitude of useless things in our shed that a good man didn't like taking something without giving something back.

It seemed a simple statement then. I was admiring an electric coffeepot with a severed cord, thinking it would be good for my cousins' playhouse.

"Remember that," Dad said.

———

To this day, I can evoke Duchess's silky coat. It floated like creek water beneath my palm, her brown eyes cautiously watching and frowning with gratitude, a crust of dried bread as good as a bone to her. Aubrey and I were soon bathing our new dog with dish detergent and the garden hose, and then brushing her coat with Mom's silver hairbrush. We loved her instantly, but Duchess ran on the road, and Mom feared her being struck by a speeding car. Her fear of the road had intensified since Aubrey and I had almost been struck a year earlier when returning from our cousins.

Hand in hand, we were licking vanilla ice-cream cones that Aunt Ruth had given to us, when a car came roaring out of nowhere. The day was steamy hot. It occurred to me later that perhaps the car had risen up through the mirage that hovered over the hot pavement, from the very depths of hell, materializing like an image in a nightmare. Seeing the car race toward us, I froze in the middle of the road, squeezing Aubrey's hand as the roaring car squealed, and then stopped dead, its rusty chrome grill almost kissing the cone that Aubrey held trembling out in front of him. His terrified closed-eyed reflection appeared in the chrome grill. He looked old and wrinkled, shellacked with the resin of fear. I heard his ice-cream cone crack. Silly how we think a held-out ice-cream cone or squinting our eyes will keep us from being harmed. Silly, how we think we can hide in our very selves, afraid.

Within moments, Mom stood beside us, her hands held to her gaping mouth, the front of her red ruffled apron covered with a dusting of flour. The driver backed up, and then slowly continued on, shaking his head, as if to say what stupid children we were. I recognized him as a man who had once come to our door to sell Dad a box of cracked Christmas ornaments. He wore a dark patch over one eye.

When his car sped away, all the sounds were gone; no *oh, sweet Canada* birds or distant chain saws, no cars arriving or departing, not a breath was heard until Mom dropped her hands down around Aubrey and made a desperate gasp. It sounded like a last breath. Until then, it was as if all our sounds had floated up and disappeared. Perhaps, someday astronauts floating in space will hear them.

Aubrey pulled away from Mom, flung his broken cone in the ditch, and then ran home. The white glop of ice cream lay melted on the road between us. It was as if a giant egg had dropped and splattered there. For the shortest moment, I imagined Mom as the mother bird and me as the mismatched egg in the nest. Her frowning eyes created a deep vertical crevice in her forehead. Her white-floured hands were crossed over her chest the way a dead person's might be. She said nothing, just turned and walked away as solemnly as a mourner from a loved one's grave. The sweet smell of vanilla wafted in the steamy heat and sickened me.

That night I woke to Mom kneeling beside my bed, crying. Her head was bowed and her hands covered her eyes. I suppose the almost-accident kept running over in her mind just as it did in mine. Something told me she was not only crying, but praying, too, and I wondered why. What was her petition? Was it one of thankfulness, or was she asking forgiveness? And was the forgiveness for me or for her? After all, I was in charge of Aubrey. I was to take his hand and watch carefully whenever we crossed the road together. And had she done the same thing at Aubrey's bedside? I listened to her sorrow, keeping my eyes closed and trying not to move. Suddenly, I felt for her the same way I felt for the gloomy-faced Sunday school children. In that moment, I did not want the responsibility of loving her.

In the morning, I rubbed my hand over the damp sheet where Mom's tears had fallen. Without the dampness, I would have considered it all a bad dream. Like the near-accident the day before, it seemed too hauntingly real to take in, even though it replayed and replayed—the hellish image rising up and speeding toward us. It seemed too overpowering to comprehend, too frightening for me to move.

A few weeks after Duchess had been given away to the Dodsons, Dad drove Aubrey and me up over the hill to visit. We missed her desperately, but Mom thought it better she live on a farm where she could run freely. Duchess, like Aubrey and me, had almost been struck by a speeding car. After, she skulked into our yard, glancing back at the road as if it were the tongue of Lucifer.

Now, her half-chewed ball lay forlorn in the corner of our verandah, her silver water bowl upside down beside it. Aubrey and I had not said this to one another, but I know we both harbored the wish to retrieve Duchess. In case we needed to catch her, I had secretly shoved a rope under the front seat of the car. To us, her return would have been as newsworthy as finding an alien in our yard.

When we pulled into the Dodsons' circular driveway, next to the dusty tractor, Duchess was conspicuously absent. No jumping on the car to greet us or barking from inside the old farmhouse. Beyond the tall leaning barn that blocked the sun were rusty-colored cows grazing. One looked our way, methodically chewing her cud, reminding me of an old-timer contemplating salvation after an altar call. Beyond the cows, down in the field, the three brothers were mending a fence.

Inside, we visited, but no one spoke of Duchess. No one seemed to dare. Our fear ruled over our words. It was a paste as thick as the sour farm smell in their kitchen, the tart smell of vinegary milk. What if Duchess had been struck, dying on the lonely road where few passed?

Mr. Dodson talked about the hot weather, the withered green beans on their vines, and the heifer cows that meandered in the field behind their house, while Aubrey wandered about admiring the piles of things that cluttered their kitchen. It seemed that many hungover men had knocked on their door, and there, too, the remnants of their broken lives had been collected.

Mrs. Dodson nodded, smiling that *yes, yes, yes*. It was not as innocuous as it was in church, but seemed too much for the cluttered vinegary space, and rather morbid. Her chubby body looked paralyzed in the armchair, her small hands crossed, her tiny feet hanging, a smile frozen upon her nodding face. I imagined her head falling from her body. I imagined it rolling away into a corner the way the toy dog's had in the back of that car window. Then, I saw her as the opposite of all things mythic. I saw her as mundane, but could not have expressed that then. And thinking back now, it would not be the mundane as in a humdrum existence, but rather the mundanity of her spirituality. How unremarkable it was.

While Aubrey and I climbed into the backseat, Dad took Mr. Dodson's arm. They stood in front of the car, facing one another, first one speaking and then the other. Mr. Dodson's big hands rolled in unison in front of him like sputtering wings trying to take flight.

In the end, Dad looked off to the road and shook his head the way I had only seen him do a few times before. Once, when Mom told him that Aubrey and I had almost been struck by a speeding car, and another time, when he heard that Stephen had been strapped by his teacher.

Dad walked to the car and got in. Mr. Dodson stepped slowly back, slipping his giant hands into his pockets as if there was something on them that he didn't want us to see, perhaps palm lines cut so jaggedly deep that they indicated cruelty, or murder, or both.

Dad never looked at Mr. Dodson again. Maybe he had dreamed of retrieving Duchess, too. He simply sped on around the circular driveway and left. I wanted to ask if Duchess had been run over, but couldn't. Neither could Aubrey, who sat with his head down, a stolen marble held like an evil eye in his palm. Halfway home, I leaned up behind Dad and tapped his shoulder. I'd been thinking of him saying that a good man didn't like taking something for nothing.

"We gave Duchess to Mr. Dodson," I said. "What did he give back to us?"

"Not a thing," Dad said, sticking a cigarette at the corner of his mouth, and then popping open his silver lighter to light it. He took a deep drag and then blew out a long stream of smoke. "Not a goddamn thing."

I leaned back and looked at Aubrey, who still sat with his palms open, the marble gone, hidden away as if it had never been there. His palms were white and smooth, looking like the ice cream that had splattered on the pavement when we had almost been struck.

Years later while rummaging in our shed, I will find a large matchbox with that marble, along with the skeleton key that he'd taken from the asylum on a day that we visited a beloved aunt. Looking at them, I knew they mirrored a matchbox in his mind, one that he had tried to ignore, or perhaps even peered into the same way that I had once peered into my uncle's maimed throat. *Anytime you go back, the familiar underpulse will start its throbbing: Home, home! And the hole torn and patched over will gape unseen again.*

When Dad was dying, I asked about Duchess. Not because she reigned supreme in my mind any longer, but because it was the middle of the night, and Dad and I were going over lots of things. Some part of us knew our talks would soon end, but we were still unwilling to admit it. His death was a terrible threat speeding toward us, one in which we had all squeezed our eyes shut in hopes that luck might save him.

Dad said that Mr. Dodson had shot Duchess.

"Why?" I breathed, the *Why* coming out of me like a lone desperate call, a sound that circled high above, and then disappeared like the sounds of the near-accident day, instilling the same loneliness that I'd felt as I watched Mom walk away from me with her hands crossed over her chest.

"Said he couldn't keep her off the road." Dad looked away.

"I thought Mr. Dodson was a Christian," I said, infuriated, the taste of vinegary milk coming up in my throat, the taste of injustice.

Dad's green eyes sat on hollow cheeks, and his once-velvety lips were now parched and downward. It seemed that loneliness was pulling on them.

"It's not beneath some misled Christians to do something bad, because they think it will keep something bad from happening."

I sat in the chair and put my head down, his statement too much for me to take in. One, where in the vision of a dog's murder, the entire world's heartache was being revealed in one person's mundanity. Mr. Dodson hadn't even attempted to be a conduit for God's love. Instead, he had let his actions begin with him. I saw the word of him carved ineptly on my childhood tree: *Sinner.*

Dad reached out and smoothed my hair, and then squeezed and rubbed my ear. I moved closer and laid my head on his chest. He patted my cheek as his breathing rattled in his chest like a tin toy. I knew behind it, a heart as strong as a boy's beat. It was then that my tears fell. The amount was not enough to wash his entire body, as my grandfather's had been when he cared for my dead grandmother, but as I cried, a river of love and understanding seemed to gush from Dad, a love so pure as to represent the Godly. It poured from him, a strong and steady stream that definitely flowed from a greater source. It enveloped me. And of course, that was it—that was what Mom had said about love. It can't begin with you.

I'd read that a miracle can only be the resurrection of love beside the unchanged fact of death. That is what I felt. A resurrection. A miracle. Perfect love and understanding coming from Dad's worn-out body, welling in me, and then dripping and pooling in the teary lake beneath us. A lake that could have been dry and barren, had it not been spiked with eternal waters, had Dad chosen to not be a conduit. And of course, I also felt the horrifying unchanged fact of death.

I never told Mom what happened to Duchess. She lived fearing the accidental and untimely death of her loved ones, and of our animals, too. This was her *afraid*. An unavoidable trait when you lose both parents at the age of two. How much worse the knowledge of a premeditated death would have been for her. Worse, I think, would have been the murderous action taken by a so-called fellow Christian. She had dedicated too much to the cause to be disappointed by a comrade who hadn't even attempted to channel love. Why had Mr. Dodson not simply given Duchess back to us? We loved her so.

Long after Dad had fallen asleep, he woke and asked me to help him to the bathroom. Determinedly, he pulled himself up, letting his now thin legs drop down, and then he smoothed his straight hair that was still more black than white, still as shiny as a young husband's coming through a back door.

I knelt to help him with his leather slippers, shaped like everyday loafers. His feet were white and cool to touch, and they reminded me of Mom's floury hands on that day of the near-accident, of the way they might look in death. In that moment, all of God's reassurances regarding death amounted to no more than a thimble-full of tainted water. There was nothing to soothe the thought that throbbed in my throat. Dad was leaving.

Dad held onto his intravenous pole like a staff, wheeling it along as I steadied his other side. Often in the night while he slept, a nurse would put a new bag of fluids on the pole. Waking in the chair, I'd watch her change the depleted bag for a plump one. Once in the dim light, it looked as if she were placing a newborn on a cross. As she left the palliative care room, I glimpsed a hazy parade of patients in johnny gowns following her, all of them wheeling a staff shaped like a cross. A procession of passing. I blinked and they departed.

Even tied tightly, Dad's ochre-colored pajama bottoms kept falling from him, yet he moved steadily, all those years of trekking through the forest now paying off by way of reserved strength. Cruising: *to travel at a steady speed*. I knew he was bravely moving toward the deathly image that raced toward him. He was no longer going to hold his hands out in front of him, or squint his eyes shut and hope for a miracle, or hide in himself, afraid. He faced his destiny like a soldier steadily moving toward a fated battle. He prepared to march with the others. In the future another dozing daughter keeping company with her dying dad may glimpse him in a procession of passing.

I opened the bathroom door and the bright fluorescent light shone out. Dad moved on alone with the pole's wheels rattling, the white light beaming through his pajama bottoms like the sun lighting up a field of goldenrod, revealing his emaciated body and curving hip bones. I even thought I glimpsed his cancer-ravaged spine missing. Dear Jesus. What rapine the cancer had wrought. He winced. Only then did I begin to feel how much he must be suffering, my brave and loving dad. Waiting on him by the closed door, my chest sank in like a grave and then swelled as wide as a tarn. It swelled with the feeling of pure love.

When he was back in his bed, I folded the white sheet over his chest. He was struggling to breathe.

"Dad," I cried, "you're suffering so."

He rested his hands on his chest. They were bony now, and his golden wedding band was as thin as wire, and loose.

"It's not the suffering," he said with labored breath. "It's not even the dying. It's the leaving."

The unchanged fact of death.

I crawled in beside him, our bodies intertwining like a suckering shrub. Finally, each breath he took matched mine. It was then that I asked him to sing "A Bicycle Built for Two." It was a song he often sang to Mom, and I thought it might make him feel stronger. In that moment I hoped more than I had ever hoped for anything that he might live, that what we glimpsed in front of us was no more than a mirage, a nightmare.

Dad started to sing, but then his voice cracked, and so I finished the verse while he tapped its tune on my arm, his breathing still labored and smelling like a rose. *But you'll look sweet upon the seat of a bicycle built for two.*

The next day, I returned home to my family in Maine for a two-day respite.

The next night Evangeline called to say Dad was gone.

Oh no. I blinked and he departed. Gone. My hands were afire as I ran through the house—down the front stairs and then up the back, all the way to the attic, and then down again—up and down until I crumbled on the kitchen floor, my mind trembling over those last moments with Dad, united in pure love and understanding—gone.

There, the black crude of obituary seeped its oily print.

What I didn't know then was that Dad's history was stamped in me. I was connected to him through our shared DNA. By God, I was connected, which meant I not only had his love and joy printed on the page of me, but the dark smudges of his fears and heartaches as well, just as I had Mom's and all our family's mothers and fathers before them. I was created from their winds.

seven

$\mathcal{A}$ friend told me that when you lose your second parent, it cancels out the loss of the first. After Mom died, no matter how hard I tried to remember Dad's face in death, I could not. I had slipped a photo of Georgia and me inside Dad's suit jacket, over his deceased heart, but what suit was he wearing, what tie, what did he look like in death? I had no recollection. In memory, his deathly face had blurred as if in watery shadow, but after my mother's death, she returned again and again. She lay beside me at night and woke me in the morning. She whispered my name and touched my shoulder. Turning to see her proved futile. There was no one there. In those empty moments, I recalled standing beside her open casket with Evangeline, who cried and said, What have they done to her mouth? Mom's mouth never looked like that.

Our mother's lips appeared smashed flat and held in a straight line, bordering on determination, but also suggesting something other; an assault was all that came to mind. I tried to push the thought away, but months later, while taking a hospice course, I would find the answer to my sister's question. While touring an undertaker's lair, a windowless basement room smelling as acrid as cat urine and resembling a torture chamber, I learned that our mother's blood had been drained from her body as if she were a slaughtered doe. After, she was bathed in chemicals and injected with formaldehyde. Then, her once-full lips, perhaps already surrendering to rigor mortis, were wrestled and stitched shut from the inside. Thus, the suggestion of her determination, and thus my perception of an assault. I recalled Evangeline's question—*What have they done to her mouth?*—and Mom's splayed and coerced lips, and then collapsed on the undertaker's floor.

When I opened my eyes, the undertaker, a pale, plump, and perspiring man, was bent over me.

"Happens all the time," he said, grinning, his jowls falling around his face like kneaded dough.

Those lips comforted me.

"What?"

Those lips were the first to kiss me.

"Yes, well, let's get you back upstairs. A Coke will do you a world of good."

For reasons I have only begun to understand, I did not want to go back upstairs to those red-carpeted receiving rooms with their faux finishes, imitation black leather chairs, and wobbly collapsible stands for flowers. Flowers that quickly droop despite their high price tag, their sickly rose scent slithering about the mourners like a warning.

NO. I wanted to stay in the torture chamber, the lair of assault, a room just like the one Mom had been in, where the last of all things vital had been drained from her, the hollow of her filled with poison, and then those reassuring mother lips wrestled and stitched closed forever. What finality. What loss.

eight

Loss. One only need glimpse Mom's life briefly to see its beginning. One only need read her journals. When she was two, her mother went to church and died. A few months later, her father went into the forest and died. It must have seemed that someone was always departing, her young life already full of cautionary tales. *If you go into the woods today, you better not go alone.*

When Mom was four, two of her older sisters climbed onto a steam train heading south—like so many other New Brunswick girls—shipped out as maids to homes of wealthy Bostonians, their apple cheeks aglow, their home-sewn skirts and blouses lined with farewell notes of blessings and warnings. Often, Mom recounted them leaving on the Canadian Pacific train, and how all of her siblings had stood in a gaggle, watching the train disappear. By then their parents had died and their family home had been seized by creditors. Mom said her oldest brother hung onto her hand to keep her from running after the train, his beautiful baritone voice, yet to be ravaged by cancer, assuring her, They won't be gone long, dear heart.

A windy, warm, September day, the Saint John River had brilliant blue waves, which Mom said was unusual. It too seemed to want to run after them. Both sisters loved the river. They had swum in it all their lives, each had been baptized in it, each had done their homework beside it, and each had taken their sorrow to its edges. Mom said they lowered their passenger window and stuck their heads out. They were wearing matching straw hats and smiling what Mom called smiles of opportunity and hope. Their tanned arms were waving. "Don't forget to swim in the river for me," Ginny had yelled above the train's chugging.

And then the train traveled around the bend and they were off with their picnic of roast turkey sandwiches and lemon cake and thermos of King Cole tea, and their Honeycrisp apples that had been picked by Mom that morning, as she sat and reached from her brother's broad shoulders and he said, *An apple a day keeps the doctor away.*

The train traveled along the river, over the border and south through fields of Maine potato plants, past the sandy beaches of New Hampshire and then to Massachusetts, where Boston waited, the city that promised them good wages for their hard work, the city that promised to reward their desire to help their orphaned family back home, a desire that had abruptly thwarted their studies to be teachers. Once ensconced as parlor maids, they would write long letters home, while tucked in the sparse servant quarters of lovely homes on the North Shore of Boston, homes that they said were lessons in luxury. Regularly, they mailed family care packages, especially to Mom, little dresses and coats and hats from Filene's Basement and saltwater taffy from Revere Beach. Regularly, whenever my mother heard the train, she would rush to the window, hoping they had returned to surprise her. Many years later, they would mail a wedding dress for Mom, a creamy satin cut on the bias that to this day is still touched and admired for its rich fabric and style, its embodiment of hope. There is a photo of Mom standing in that wedding dress, looking out a window that faced the train tracks.

Once a year, the sisters traveled back on that same train for a summer holiday, crying when they arrived and crying when they swam and then walked along the river, before having to return to Boston. Later, Marguerite would marry and have five little boys in succession, her life turning for the worse when her husband, said to be a lovely man, shot himself in their family car. After finding him, she had a nervous breakdown. When word came of this double tragedy, Uncle Rand went to retrieve those five little boys, boarding the same train that his sisters had boarded years earlier, traveling along the Saint John River and then south through fields of Maine potatoes, past the sandy beaches of New Hampshire, and then to Massachusetts, where Boston waited. Arriving in New Brunswick with fresh haircuts and doe-colored eyes, the boys were divided among their relatives to be cared for until their mother could recover.

Much later when word came of Ginny's advanced cancer, Uncle Rand once again took that train, only to find her already in the morgue when he arrived. After, he went to her apartment to gather and pack her things, but the landlord had already evicted Ginny and moved another woman in. Her belongings were stacked in wet cardboard boxes with the trash behind a back shed, the ink of her farewell notes, the blessings and warnings, seeping the same blue as her beloved Saint John River. Uncle Rand returned with his sister in a casket, no more letters, no more smiles of opportunity and hope, her beautiful lips having been stitched shut forever.

Studying the family photo albums, I often asked Mom, "What kind of cancer did Ginny have?" *Had she not eaten her apple a day?*

Mom didn't seem to know, or perhaps she didn't want to say or be reminded. Of course, I'd eavesdropped over the years and pieced some things together, but I wanted her to tell me the whole story from beginning to end. I wanted her version, her narrative to live in me just as it lived in her, not understanding then that it already did.

"Why did Aunt Marguerite have a nervous breakdown?"

I studied a picture of her standing in front of her pretty front door, holding her last baby. She looked tired and her hair was not styled as it was in other photos. To me, she looked resigned and also sad, as if she had glimpsed their future. Perhaps even more ominous was that in the corner of the photo was the front fender of their family car, looking so huge that it seemed to diminish everything else in the photograph, even Marguerite and her baby.

"Mom, why did Aunt Marguerite have a nervous breakdown?"

Again, Mom acted as if she didn't really know, or perhaps she didn't want to say or be reminded. The message in her eyes said that young girls left for distant places and then bad things happened.

What loss.

When I was fifteen, my school organized a trip to Italy. My feelings of unsettlement had intensified with puberty, and I desperately wanted to go. Several times while doing homework at the kitchen table, I'd mentioned the trip to my parents without much response. Mom listened for a moment, but then continued humming while cooking or washing dishes, while Dad peered around his newspaper for only a second and then continued reading. I studied his tanned fingers holding the *Daily Gleaner*, sooty with newsprint and dusted with the political events he adored. His hope for all of us lay with Prime Minister Trudeau and the Liberal Party, and he knew their philosophies as well as he knew the words to "O Canada." One only need say the word *Tory* to make him swear, of which Mom disapproved. Looking back, I am not sure whether it was his swearing or her conservative leanings that caused her disapproval. I only know that sometimes I incited Dad—Those Tories are at it again, Dad—just to incite Mom.

Assholes, he'd say.

Gordon, please.

But that night, I was careful to avoid such dustings. The down payment for the trip was due the following day, and Dad had just returned from visiting his ill brother in Connecticut, his lips drawn, yet his mood as always, kind toward us. After reminding Dad, he folded his newspaper, retrieved his checkbook, and then wrote a check across from me at the kitchen table. It was as if he had made his decision long ago and only needed to be reminded.

Drying her hands on her apron, Mom began her rebuttal, and I feared her influence. With matters of their children, Dad almost always conceded—not because he feared her, but rather, I think, he feared her intuition, its shocking and accurate precision constantly confirmed.

"I'm not so sure we should send her over there alone," Mom said. *If you go into the woods today, you better not go alone.*

"She's not going alone. She's going with her classmates and two chaperones." Dad handed me the check, which I snatched, folded, and shoved in my jeans pocket.

"But it's so far. What if she gets sick?"

"She's got to go sometime," Dad said.

"Why? Why does she have to go sometime?" Mom's forehead was wrinkled and her eyes questioning. I knew her sisters' destinies were still as thick as honey in the comb of her, but I wasn't going off to work as a parlor maid, I was going on a school trip to learn about another culture. Mom looked at me, her blue eyes searching mine, love imprinted on them like the lyrics of a dirge for lost girls. I thought I saw a tear shimmering, even though she had stopped crying years before.

"I can't cry anymore," she confessed when she heard that Uncle Rand would lose his voice to larynx cancer, the voice that had comforted her as she'd watched her sisters depart. "It's too much. I wish I could." Cried out, is what she called it.

I had gotten in the habit of crying for her, a practice that would serve me well later when I tried my hand at acting, and an idea that I'd gotten from reading about the paid mourners in Dickens. It was easy. I only needed to think of Pony or Duchess or Stephen on the night that he was shot, or recall Mom when bad news arrived, her face becoming so locked in grief that my tears surrendered quickly. I didn't want a sad-looking mother. I also feared her sadness permeating the comb of me, a grievous honey that might last forever, like the honey in King Tut's tomb. In those times, I longed for Mom's pretty and fluid face, and I knew my tears would speed up its return. But that day, check in pocket, I looked away from her. I did not want to cry. I was happy and hopeful, and I was going to Rome.

"Look on the bright side," Dad said, returning to his La-Z-Boy and newspaper. "She'll come back with some good stories."

My storytelling, the very thing they both took pride in, Mom often complimenting me on my art of embellishment, while Dad called it for the outright lying that it was. Storytelling. Dad had placed it between them like an offering, even though I am sure it felt like a wishbone to Mom. Whoever pulled the hardest would surely lose.

Dad swiveled in his chair and looked at Mom, and then nodded the same encouraging nod he often gave to her on Election Day, when counseling her to vote for the Liberal Party, for the sake of our family. *Damn Tories. If they get half a chance, they'll ruin the country.*

Mom shook her head, glancing at me as if to say, I give in. I'd like to say she smiled before turning away, but I truly can't recall.

I do recall Dad glancing at me and winking. Not to suggest that we'd gotten away with something, for he never sided with any of us against Mom, but in a way that said, You are a good girl. Go on and enjoy yourself.

A few weeks later, Mom delivered to my bedroom a pamphlet on the white slave trade, evidently alive and well in foreign countries, and a small belt with a large pocket that she had been sewing that afternoon. At first, I thought it might be a pocket for my farewell notes—blessings and warnings—or a chastity belt, like the one that I'd read about in the book of modern myths. Its listed uses were to prevent rape or temptation, and the juxtaposition of those two very different meanings had sealed the belt's image in my mind. Was Mom worried about how dangerous or tantalizing those Italian boys might be? I must have blushed with this thought, because she tilted her head questioningly.

"It's for your passport," she said. "You wear it under your clothing so your identification is always with you. No matter what."

No matter what?

This was Mom looking on the bright side, and obviously she was imagining a far different Italy than I. I'd been admiring a history book on Rome that my teacher and future chaperone, Miss Flowers, had loaned to me. Usually, Miss Flowers, a young sexy number, solicited scorn from my girlfriends and me, because she flirted with senior boys, but the book had momentarily redeemed her. Leafing through it, I had settled on the Colosseum as my fantasy setting. I imagined myself wandering through the ancient ruins, my skin tanned like my aunts' when they left on the train for Boston. I saw my long straight hair suddenly curly, as if I were of Italian descent, wearing a ruffled white peasant dress, with a jangling coin necklace and earrings, similar to a costume that I had seen Sophia Loren wear in a late-night movie. Behind me, a chorus of Italian boys followed, singing "Waterloo."

I glanced up. Mom was looking at me, but also through me, her blue eyes still carrying a tinge of that dirge for lost girls. It was a look she often had while folding laundry or washing dishes, or kneading bread dough. I looked away, taking my fresh passport from its newly sewn home and rubbing the golden letters, CANADA.

"Thanks, Mom. Thanks for sewing this for me. And don't worry. I'll be careful."

She took my passport, opened it, and studied my photograph.

"You don't realize how pretty you are. Sometimes that attracts the wrong kind." She sighed. "You remind me of Ginny."

I looked down and fingered a hole as round as the letter *o* in my blue jeans. Had Ginny attracted the wrong kind of people? I recalled a photo of her sitting with Dad and two of my siblings on one of her visits home. Everything about her was pretty—her tanned legs and arms, her hands and shirtdress, her perky satisfied lips, much like my mother's. Attractiveness radiated from her, and she seemed comfortable, self-assured.

I knew that Mom was finally offering me the narrative that I longed for, but I refused it, because in that moment, I was no longer sure that I wanted it. What if the sadness of it overtook me, or within it, there was a responsibility?

"Ginny's hair was reddish-blonde," I said. "And mine is black."

"But you really do resemble her," Mom insisted.

"My friends say I look like Cher." I told her how they laughed and cheered when I tucked a crow's feather behind my ear and sang, *Half-breed*, bloating my cheeks out as if they were full of acorns.

Mom didn't respond, and that weighed on me. I looked at my Frye boots that were leaning against my dresser. They, too, made a compelling juxtaposition, the gleaming white dresser and the worn and wrinkled brown leather. Something about it seemed timely, and also irretrievably innocent, but I didn't know why.

"Don't worry, Mom," I finally said. "I won't be gone long."

A few days later, Mom returned from our local department store with new Levis and yellow cotton pajamas covered with blue fleur-de-lis, the latter surely her cosmopolitan nod to me. Such fabric designs were new to both of us, and adored by the French families who had recently come from Quebec to live in rows of prefab houses and work at the newly erected paper mill. Fleur-de-lis appeared on their children's T-shirts and sweatshirts, and even tattooed on the thick arms of some fathers in muscle shirts, which like the prefab houses and French-speaking families were also new to us. These same muscle-shirted fathers also wore teeny-weeny Speedos when they came to the river or lake to swim, a sight that prompted my girlfriends and me to roll over on our towels and blurt out with laughter. We were at that age, which found not only merciless humor but ridicule in the unfamiliar customs and habits of others. *What a getup.*

A gang of five girls—Sheryl, Laurie, Patty, Mona, and I—we sometimes turned our mean and cutting remarks on one another, especially if anyone hinted at defection by way of aloofness or a strong contrary opinion. Although we were allowed small differences with our choices of hairstyle and fashion, for the most part, we were to think alike and disclose all secrets, a necessary tactic used to encourage loyalty to the greater cause, the gang. Otherwise, our force might be diminished, especially at school.

Sometimes the girls smothered me as much as my mother, and I longed to set out on my own. I longed to be a private person. I'd become interested in sex despite being as green as a fiddlehead, and although I reported embellished stories of getting hot and heavy, as the gang called it, I wasn't sure that I would be able to bring myself to report the true and real deal, if it should ever happen. Unbeknownst to my comrades, I was desperate to gain experience, and my plan was to eventually rid myself of my virginity, even flirting shamelessly with some homeboys, but none had bothered to follow my lead. My forwardness seemed to worry them. I saw in their eyes a frightened and questioning thrill—*Really?*—the same look they gave to Miss Flowers when she flirted with them.

In Italy, our gang soon learned that like the Quebecois, Italians had different customs.

"Did you see the way the passport guy flirted with me?" Sheryl gleamed as we exited the Rome airport, a disheveled herd of teenagers and two chaperones, weighed down with recently searched luggage and squinting at the rising sun.

"He did not flirt with you," I said.

Sheryl stopped, her blue eyes lit with foreign light.

"Well, why else would he say ooh-la-la while fondling my clothes?"

"Beats me," I said, although I surmised it might have been from viewing her matching sets of bras and panties. Red, white, and blue—the same trio of colors as her T-shirts and sweater collections, the same as her striped bedroom wallpaper back home—those were Sheryl's colors, from which she never deviated. A distinction we girls allowed, but often criticized.

"I think he likes me," Sheryl confessed.

"I think he saw all that matching underwear and thought you were a hooker."

Behind us, Laurie and Patty and Mona laughed.

"Ooh-la-la, the Happy Hooker," cackling the title of the book that we were all dying to read, but were too ashamed to buy.

Sheryl slapped my head and I made a fake cry. Miss Flowers stopped ahead of us and turned, her teased blonde hair now messed, making her look like a cartoon character that had stuck her finger in a socket. Her look somehow held the feeling of desperation, and it took a moment to realize that she was glaring at us. We had interrupted her ongoing conversation with a senior named John, a muscle-bound farm boy with excellent manners. Miss Flowers had traded her seat to sit next to him on the flight, an action brought to the gang's attention by an anonymous catcall. For the rest of the flight, we took turns spying on them, and then reporting back to one another with observations and snatched snippets of their conversation.

She's purring his name and pawing him like a kitten. "Of course, I am listening, Miss Flowers. Yes, ma'am, I am. No, I'm not a bit sleepy. No, no, I don't need to share your blanket. If anything, I'm a little bit warm."

Miss Flowers hurried to catch up to John, who had no doubt seen the moment as his get-away opportunity, and we girls followed on, singing low while watching them, *Here's to you Mrs. Robinson, Jesus loves you more than you could know, whoa, whoa, whoa. Oh here's to you. . . .*

———

Our small hotel on a narrow Rome side street was a lesson in luxury. Floor-to-ceiling windows, curtained with satin the same creamy color as my mother's wedding dress. The windows opened onto little patios that the hotel staff called the *balcone.* The walls were a darker shade of Prince Edward Island beaches, and two narrow beds were pushed together and covered with purple velvet bedspreads. Later, Miss Flowers would tell us the wall color was sienna and the bedspread aubergine, words that we girls dramatically exaggerated behind her back, as if we had finally found the perfect definitions for her sleaziness.

Still, secretly we all adored her worldliness. She told us with glittering eyes that an Italian man could pinch us. A two-finger squeeze on the bottom was considered legal, and a compliment, while a five-finger squeeze was considered to be in bad taste, and if this should happen, we were to turn and shake our finger in disapproval. Never let a man go further than he should. It's up to the woman to lead. And by the way, she added, those were not two toilets in our bathrooms as some students thought, but a toilet and a bidet. *A bidet?* Yes, if one desired, she said, one could sit and spritz their private area rather than taking a full dip in the bath. *Really?* It was rumored that one classmate, after indulging in a lumberjack portion of spaghetti, had then thrown up in his bidet, while we girls had used ours to wash and scrub our feet before giving one another pedicures.

One of the girls teased that maybe we could use the bidet to wash off the fingerprints of flirty Italians, prompting Miss Flowers to wag her finger while smiling slyly, as if she were the true leader of our gang. From then on, we valued Miss Flowers educating us, carrying on the spirit of it among ourselves, albeit in a more crude fashion:

Don't lock arms, you look like lesbos.

Black eyeliner all the way around your eye makes you look like a rabid raccoon.

Hike that skirt up one more inch and someone's gonna be passing you a five-dollar bill.

Five dollars, my ass.

That's what we said. Five dollars for your ass.

———

Our Rome mornings were full of walking tours, which we all dolled up for as if we had been given parts in an Italian movie. The cobblestone sidewalks were crowded and busy with Italian accents, punctuated with echoing church bells and tiny speeding cars. Rome smelled of baking bread and roasted chestnuts, with waves of urine from the alleys where stray and wild cats skirted. On some corners were wooden carts of tomatoes and peppers, and eggplant the same color as our hotel bedspreads.

The gang excitedly noted that boys outnumbered girls, *if* you didn't count the many widows, completely dressed in black from scarf to shoe, their faces wrinkled like the roasting chestnuts. Nuns were plentiful, too, their winged habits parting the waves of people as they walked briskly from place to place. The Italian boys flocked like crows behind us, snickering and posturing with their cans of Coke, only to all vanish by lunchtime. Soon, we learned from Miss Flowers that they had returned to their mothers—as all good Italian boys do—for huge lunches and then long siestas, before visiting their proper girlfriends, who evidently were not allowed to roam the streets like we Canadians. By evening, the boys left their proper girlfriends behind and filled the streets once again, following us as we licked our evening gelatos, giggling and ridiculing their sing-songy voices and accents. They called out their names to us, all ending in o. Antonio, Carlo, Alberto, Vito, Filippo.

Hey, where you from? they called.

Canada, someone would always confess.

Canada girls, come-a back here. We wanna talk to you.

What's your name-a? You girl with boots. Come-a back. I want to show you the sights.

Go away, *mafioso*, we shouted. It was one of the few Italian words besides *ciao* that we knew, marveling at the fact that there was one word that could be used for both hello and good-bye. How convenient, we said. The same words we had uttered to Miss Flowers after she explained the bidet to us.

Each night we let the boys come a little closer. Each night we flirted with them a little more and made fun of them a little less. Now, we rustled through our pocket dictionaries, desperately trying to translate their words. All the way back to our hotel, they followed, smoking and loitering for hours outside the gate, appearing restless and imprisoned, although the gate was never locked.

Our chaperones, one weary and one preoccupied with John, always encouraged us to go to bed early, to read and to get our rest. Off we'd go, the good-mannered homeboys to their wing and we girls to ours. Reading was not a problem, since my roommate had smuggled a copy of *The Joy of Sex* to Italy with her. After getting into pj's, the rest of our gang tiptoed down the hallway, knocking three times to signify a curious party. *Ciao*, baby, they sang in their best Italian accents while rushing in. Then, we all circled the book on the center of the aubergine bedspread like kittens around a saucer of cream.

"Weren't you afraid someone in Customs would see this?" Laurie asked.

"Sex isn't a crime," Sheryl retorted, sitting proudly in her striped red-white-and-blue pj's.

"Maybe the Customs guy saw it," Patty said. "That's what got him hot and bothered."

"Where did you get it?" We all wanted to know.

"Under my parents' mattress."

We all bowed our heads as if in church. Sex between parents being something that none of us wanted to ridicule or even envision for a moment. Instead, we chose to focus on some of the physical contortions suggested in the book, sharing our dismay at the potential lack of comfort. Who wanted to stand up or be crouched like a frightened rabbit? Who would call that joy? And besides, someone noted, the guy looks like a middle-aged greasy hippie. After thumbing through the book, the girls tired of the pictures, agreeing that they'd much rather read *The Happy Hooker*, and then drifted off to paint their nails or pluck their eyebrows, at which point I lifted the book from the bed and slinked off to a corner.

Behind me, the girls sensing a defection, made fun of my fleur-de-lis pj's, accusing me of going Quebecois, and of being madly in love with Pierre Trudeau, since they knew I followed him as closely in the newspapers as my father did. Then they accused me of being jealous of Maggie Trudeau because she got to sleep with the prime minister of Canada, and I didn't. Normally, I would have argued that it was Maggie I really admired for her freewheeling and defiant lifestyle, but I let it go.

Although there was no mention of a chastity belt in *The Joy of Sex*, the book did define the word *hymen*, alerting me again to my virginity. What a nuisance. It seemed that it would be a hindrance with a boy I actually loved, and an awkward and no doubt sentimental formality before getting down to the good stuff. I luxuriated in the thought of being put asleep and having it removed like an inflamed appendix. Done. Even the sound of the word begged avoidance. Not one of my friends had ever uttered it. It, like the suggestion of parents having sex, demanded avoidance. Reading its meaning had been enough, although to this day, I wonder why it has the word *men* in it. If I were the writer Anne Carson, I would have figured that out long ago, no doubt tying it to some ancient myth, or perhaps even to the vestal virgins who took a vow of chastity and kept the eternal fires burning at the Colosseum. What would they think of its ruin now, looming like an abandoned and broken honeycomb?

Near the end of our time in Rome, we girls had all matched up with a boy from the *mafiosi*, prompting us to adopt the name-ending *o* for ourselves. Debbie-o Sheryl-o, Laurie-o, Patty-o, Mon-o. Mono. *You're not calling me Mono.*

But we did.

Mono and Carlo up in a tree, passing their germs like greasy hippies.

Now in the evenings after some handholding and parting pecks on our cheeks, the Italian boys peered like starved prisoners from the other side of the hotel's gate. Sometimes, we gathered on the *balcone* and mimicked them. Sometimes we threw kisses like Sophia Loren. When they called out, we again flipped through our Italian dictionaries, trying to decipher their messages. Frustrated in our search, we often called random phrases back to them: *Dove possiamo andare a ballare?* Where can we go dancing? *C'è una pista di pattinaggio qui vicino?* Is there a skating rink near here? *Cosa desidera?* What would you like?

On our second-to-last night, Antonio came to the balcony door. Sheryl had just turned off the light when we heard his gentle knocking. It sounded like a hummingbird pecking. We opened the door to find him sitting on the railing, grinning. The moon made his teeth gleam like river water.

"Debbie," he said. "Come with me."

I looked at Sheryl and she at me, and then I signaled for him to wait before closing the door.

"Are you going to go?" Sheryl whispered, looking at me as if I were about to betray her.

I nodded yes before going to the bathroom and hooking my passport belt under my pajamas. Catching myself in the mirror, I saw that my cheeks were flushed the color of apples, which made me picture my aunts leaving on the train. For a moment, I hesitated, but then I retrieved my boots and jean jacket and put them on, picturing myself as free as Maggie Trudeau.

"What should I say if someone comes looking for you while you're off with Romeo?" Sheryl had turned the lamp on and was back in her bed, flipping through her Italian dictionary.

"No one will," I said.

She slammed the dictionary shut and threw it hard against the sienna-colored wall. I had a vision of all the words tumbling from the book, its pages turning as plain and white as a young girl's skin.

"Well, Debbie-o," she said, "I am not going to lie for you."

"Fine," I said.

Outside, the night was cool and the pine trees with their great crowns were silhouetted by the moonlight. Antonio took my hand and then stood back, looking at my pj's.

"French?" he asked.

"No," I said, feeling my cheeks flush deeper.

Somewhere in the distance, a dog barked, and a bird that sounded like an owl cooed. *Who?* The night smelled of lilies and of rain, with hints of diesel oil.

"We walk." Antonio smiled. His smooth-looking hair was as shiny as crow feathers, and he was tall, wearing bell-bottom jeans and a yellow V-neck sweater. I couldn't help noting that the boys from home would never wear such a getup, and that lone detail somehow made things even more exciting.

He took my hand. "I take you."

And with that we hopped over the railing of the *balcone*.

The night from there on is no longer clear in my memory, or maybe it never was. I know that I did not lead as Miss Flowers had instructed, although that had been my intention. In retrospect, I see how naive I was regarding my ability for persuasion. This may be the curse of girls who are so loved at home. They are somehow unprepared for the world, even with their mother's warnings. I know that after a while, my cadence became a little less confident, and that I often checked to make sure that my passport was still snug against me. No matter what.

I know that Antonio seemed excited as he led me through a maze of side streets, and that the streets were mostly empty and mostly smelled musty, and that the dim gaslights reflected on the streets like white puddles. Antonio glanced at me, often smiling and squeezing my hand, and when he leaned close to me and spoke, I smelled a tinge of sulfur like the paper mill back home. Years later, I would identify it as fresh garlic, something foreign then to my mother's pantry, except for dried garlic salt that tasted neither of salt nor garlic.

Eventually we ended up at the Colosseum, which in the moonlight looked harsher than a crumpled honeycomb, and more like a large broken crown. My class had toured it the day before. Then, it had seemed like a defeated spot, but now in the moonlight, it looked much larger and seemed to hold a certain power. For a long time, Antonio and I stood looking at it as if it represented a new world to both of us, and for the shortest second we seemed united. I thought of all the animals and people that had died and there rose a mist in the night that I would later view as the spirit of everything innocent rising. I pictured slaves and animals slaughtered for the sake of entertainment, panthers and apes and giraffes, elephants and jaguars and wild horses, so many that after, some were deemed to be extinct. Later, I would obsess about the hunts and executions and battles that had taken place, and for a time back home with my family, I would recite the massacres, some invented and embellished, some pointed out in Miss Flowers's book on Rome, which I never returned.

Antonio led me beneath an archway and then moved quickly, as familiar with the ruins as a wild cat that had always lived there. Touching the broken walls as I passed left a dust like flour on my hands. Antonio pointed out certain spots and gestured in Italian, at what I wasn't sure, and although I didn't lose my virginity that night, I did end up in what I now recall, many years later, as a struggle that left me damp and dirty. Albeit neither rape nor temptation, in those moments, I would have gladly exchanged my passport belt for a chastity belt. I tried to be accommodating as if an actor in a reenactment, and thankfully, my suitor was almost as inexperienced as I. Still, the combination of his actions and my own submissiveness left me feeling soiled and condemned. For what, I wasn't really sure. It seemed that I had traveled back to another time when a woman, like the animals, had little recourse. In those moments, it did not seem that I lived in the same time as Maggie Trudeau, who hung out with Castro and partied with the Rolling Stones. It seemed rather that I had been given a part in some cautionary tale. It was then that I remembered Mom tempting me with Aunt Ginny's story, the story that I had refused. What in me reminded Mom of Ginny? And why had I not kept my promise to her to be careful?

During the struggle, I had cried, *Cosa desidera?* What would you like? Something that still shames me. Perhaps because even while saying it, I knew I was denying what was really happening. After all, Antonio's hand was against my breastbone and pushing me down and his shape in the moonlight resembled a great falcon, even the crook of his nose. I wanted to scream, but I knew my scream would only be an echo there. Years later, I would read that all aggression, whether it comes from man or from the world, is of animal nature, the phrase catapulting me back to those moments in Rome. Even the abrupt smell of garlic returned.

That night I closed my eyes so as not to see him over me. The word *venatores* from the book on Rome came to me, a term given to the gladiators who killed the wild beasts. I recalled that fleeing ostriches were decapitated with crescent-shaped arrows, and that some animals were even taught to do tricks before they were slaughtered. Little dogs dancing on their hind legs and begging. Now, years later, this is the detail that remains—not the slaughtering of innocence, but the detail of a taming, so to speak. I am not sure why. I only know that after, I felt as if some sentence had come upon me, one with a word as condemning as the word *thieves*, in Cher's song. *But every night all the men would come around and lay their money down.*

Disheveled and following Antonio out of the Colosseum, I thought I glimpsed a rustling white cloak moving in the shadows, perhaps a ghostly vestal virgin keeping the eternal flame burning, a ghost who could pardon me from my own sentencing. The image sustained me until on a nearby side street I saw the gang of boys—their names all ending in *o*—smoking and watching from an alleyway, their eyes glistening like paid mourners. Even from a distance, I could feel them mocking me.

Antonio pretended not to notice the boys, but in that he was also inexperienced. I knew then that I had been part of a bet, a trick, a public offering for entertainment, and I fought to keep the tears back, lifting my chin and rushing onward. Antonio acted as if no aggression had taken place. He was perfectly pleasant, but for the rest of the walk back, I feared as much as any fear I'd ever had that I was destined for the white slave trade. I longed for Mom and her warnings. I wanted more than anything to be smothered by her, to be given the chance to cry for her again. I imagined how permanently heavy her face would become if something happened to me—*what loss*—my presence like her sisters in the family photo album, my demise too much for her to ever explain.

I knew then that Mom wasn't avoiding telling me about the lives that her sisters had, but she was avoiding telling me about the lives that they hadn't, their hopes and dreams never coming true. Years later, I would find Ginny's last letter to Mom, a letter where her illness had weakened her handwriting. And even though she would die a few weeks after writing that letter, she was telling of her plan to buy a sports car and return to New Brunswick. An MG, to be exact. "I must. I miss you. I miss the river," she had written.

Antonio asked if I wanted a Coke, but I said nothing. *A Coke will do you a world of good.* He asked if I was cold. Again, I said nothing. I couldn't. When my hotel was in view, I took off running, leaving Antonio behind. He called out something in Italian. I think it had the word *brother* in it. I never looked back. Instead, I imagined that gang of o-ending names grabbing and pulling me, stealing me, taking me to a life from which I would never escape, the *venatores* having ravaged me like a wishbone.

The balcony door was locked. Maybe by accident, or maybe as Sheryl's punishment for my betrayal. And of course, she knew. This was the night that would separate us forever, although I would feign otherwise. This was the night that I left my gang behind to learn things that forbade repeating, things that repulsed me far more than certain words or images of greasy hippies making out, and in the end, my shame made an actor out of me. My shame of not being careful, as I had promised Mom, my shame of having been tricked. What a fool.

I turned and leaned against the balcony door to catch my breath. There was no one there, no white slave bandits, just the moon and the crowned trees and the cool misty night, staying with me until I could bring myself to walk around and enter through the front door of the hotel.

The lights in the foyer were dimmed and the night manager slept in his chair and snored. I reached over the desk and took the golden key for my room. Near the keys was a plant that smelled of lemons. It smelled so pure that I wanted to steal it.

Halfway down the hotel hallway, I saw John leaving Miss Flowers's room. He had his new white sneakers in his hand, and when he turned and saw me passing, he looked as sad as I felt. Something in his eyes seemed to beg my pardon, and he smiled just a bit, but I could not smile back, because my lips felt as if they had been stitched shut, or like the rest of me, they had been wrestled to conform. *Cosa desidera?*

After John passed, he whispered *Ciao*, that word we both had only recently learned. The sound of his gentle farm-boy voice made me feel as if I'd lost someone very dear. *Hello and good-bye.*

That night, I filled the bidet and sat beside it. What would it take to make me feel pure again? Perhaps more than a reassuring wink from Dad, *You are a good girl*, and more cleansing water than I could ever put in a bidet. It would be late evening back home. Saturday. Mom would be in the bath or on the sofa, reading. Earlier in the day, she would have mixed bread dough and then left it in the buttered bowl to rise up like a heavy cloud. Much later, she would have punched the dough back down and kneaded it, folding and rolling it away from her and then back, its yeastiness filling the kitchen with promise. I imagined her staring off as she always did while kneading. It seemed as if the action took her on a journey, one that was steeped with melancholy, the kind ignited by the knowledge that someone very special is and will always be missing.

I imagined Mom's hands white with flour. Had I read that the vestal virgins made a special flour that was sprinkled on the sacrifices to the gods, or had I dreamed it? The image of a fawn visited me, dusted white and standing beside a river with its head down, crying like a hurt girl.

I washed my fleur-de-lis pajamas and hung them over the bathtub like a giant flag to dry. Even though my girlfriends were sleeping all around me, I missed them just as I would from that night on. Life had begun to draw its chalky boundaries. I missed my little stretch of road, its new pulp mill and rows of prefab houses, its Quebecois, its Speedo Frenchmen, its Pierre Trudeau constantly promising change on the front pages of the *Daily Gleaner*. My father, oh Father, *O Canada*. I missed my home and my mother, her heart forever sticky with the nectar of missing loved ones. I remembered the photograph of her standing in her wedding dress. Many times, she had told me the window where she stood faced the river and the train tracks. She is holding one of her hands behind her back as if tied, and something about her appears pensive, contemplative, perhaps even sad. I felt the weight of her years watching for her sisters, and it somehow made me miss them, too, and the story of their lives that should have been. How many times had their hopes and desires been aroused? Only to crumble like a fortress.

Then, I longed more than anything to be back home, and to heed that salutation, *Swim in the river for me.*

nine

*I*n Bangor, Maine, there is a replica of the five-story brick mental hospital where my maternal grandmother died. It has stacked, barred windows identical to those her daughter, a schoolteacher, would stand in years after her mother's death, crying and clinging to the bars, her head tucked beneath one reaching arm like that of an ibis. Some of her family members who had just visited were driving away. I was in that departing car. I was seven and felt afraid for my aunt. Something about the still and paralyzed look on her face and the swirl of the yellowish-orange paint on the visiting room's walls had made me feel as if her life in that place were racing out of control.

The clammy July heat made my legs stick to the car seat, so I had turned my head only slightly to look back at my aunt. The sun was shining on the window where she stood, and it made her appear ghostly behind the bars. Earlier in the visiting room, a man with withered skin and long hair like Geronimo had put his face close to mine and stuck his tongue out. His tongue looked like the pointed tongue of a sparrow and his breath smelled both fiery and sour. The ends of his hair looked as if they had been singed by fire.

Dad drove that day. Mom sat close to him and cried. "I wish we could get her out of there. She'll die in there, just like my mother."

Dad took one hand off the steering wheel and pulled Mom close to him, which made her cry more. Her shoulders were round and white in a sleeveless paisley dress and they heaved up and down as if her heart were trying to escape. I thought Dad might sing one of the many songs he often sang to Mom while he was driving, but he was quiet. Still, I imagined him singing:
Daisy, Daisy, give me your answer, do.
I'm half-crazy, all for the love of you.

It won't be a stylish marriage,
I can't afford a carriage,
But you'll look sweet upon the seat
Of a bicycle built for two!

Aubrey sat next to me, staring down at his open palm, which held a black, skeleton key. It looked exactly like the one the nurse had used to open my aunt's locked door. I reached over to touch it, but Aubrey closed his hand quickly and stared at me as if to say, You never saw that.

I wondered if he had stolen the key to my aunt's room, or if he had taken some random key left on a table or a wooden bench in that hideous-colored waiting room. Or did one single key work for all the rooms? Could a boy steal a key, and then unlock every door, freeing the patients like birds from a cage?

"What did you think of that man?" I whispered. "The one who stuck his tongue out at me?"

"What a spook," Aubrey said, and then looked away. "They're all a bunch of spooks. Crazy as Indians."

Dad's green-blue eyes flashed in the rearview mirror. "Better not to say that," he said in a kind, but firm, manner.

Before we turned onto the main road, I looked back at the hospital. All I could see was a bright sunspot in the window where Aunt Anna had stood. It was as if she'd been zapped away and nothing was left but a bright gleaming stain. When we moved beyond the black iron gates, I saw the name of the hospital written on a plaque. FAIRVIEW.

As the road ahead twisted and curved toward home, I listened to Mom, whose outcry had turned to sighing, while I quietly recited all the provinces of Canada with their capitals, one of the many things besides reading and arithmetic that my now barred aunt had enjoyed teaching me. The capital of Nova Scotia is Halifax, the capital of Prince Edward Island is Charlottetown, the capital of Newfoundland is St. John's, the capital of New Brunswick is Fredericton . . .

When I finished all ten provinces, plus the Yukon and the Northwest Territories, I began again, for in the exercise of remembering and repeating, I could see my aunt's broad-cheeked face before me instead of the road ahead. I could see her lips, which were always plump and pretty, but had on that day resembled two dried worms.

Driving through Bucksport, Maine, to reach Castine, I pass a paper mill like the one that promised progress to our small stretch of Canadian road in the late sixties. First, heavy machinery called harvesters clear-cut a large swath of forest near the Saint John River. The machinery did not cut the trees, as was the usual custom, but yanked out every tree in its path until a whole section of forest lay decimated, the roots twisting up like arthritic hands. The decimation disturbed Dad. He knew those woods intimately, and he believed in selective cutting and replanting. He also believed in only taking what was needed, and he knew the roots of the great trees on the banks of the Saint John River held everything in place. Without them, the spring melts would bring flooding and erosion.

After the huge trees had been hauled away, a barren, dusty patch of land remained. Black crows flew and pecked about. Looking at it, I thought of Golgotha, a place that I'd heard about in church, the hill where Jesus was crucified.

In the months that followed, a high, steel building was slowly erected and then fenced in like a prison with barbed wire. One cold fall day the progress began, signified by white sulfur-smelling smoke that billowed into the blue sky. If I were to give the smell a color, it would not have been white, but the yellowish-orange of the visiting room walls at Fairview.

One Sunday beneath the smoke, a line of local men with hard hats and silver lunch pails walked behind the fence to begin their shift. Driving the family to church, Dad slowed down to watch them enter the mill, a towering gray wall of a building without windows. Aubrey leaned over the front seat and asked what they did in the mill. What did they make?

"They're making clouds," Dad said, and then he lit a cigarette. In the shadow of the great cloud-maker, the smoke my father expelled seemed wispy and insignificant.

———

Outside of Bucksport, Maine, is a long stretch of road with a railroad track crossing, much like the one where Dad's car was hit by a speeding train. He had just dropped Aubrey off at hockey practice in the new arena, paid for by the new mill, and was returning home. The moonlit night was white with crusty snow, the sky clear and starry. When the train hit Dad's car, it carried him half a mile along the tracks and into the woods before coming to a complete stop. The train tracks were also new, courtesy of the paper mill, and while speeding home, Dad completely forgot about them. Since the wigwags and warning lights had yet to be installed, there was nothing to remind him.

Afterward, Dad's new Ford LTD resembled crumpled paper. Volunteer firemen worked almost an hour before they were able to pry him out from under the dash. Fortunately, he had known enough to duck. *Jack be nimble, Jack be quick.* Rescued, he punched his wool fedora back into shape before placing it on his head, and then walked away unscathed in his forest-green car coat, as the train sat still and steaming on the tracks. Much later, he told me that the firemen wanted to drive him home, but that he thought the best thing for his nerves in those moments was to take a long walk. When I asked him why, he said because he knew he had just experienced a miracle, that he shouldn't have survived, and he needed some time to think about that.

When Dad reached the road he could hear someone calling, *Dad, Dad, Dad.* Aubrey had run three miles from the arena after someone told him that his father's car had been struck by a speeding train. Years later, Aubrey would tell me he took a shortcut across the frozen river to get to the railroad tracks.

Although snowmobiles and even cars sometimes ventured out onto the ice, we were warned to stay away. Dad said that one could never predict when a body of frozen water might open. I thought how my little brother could have disappeared into the great river that night, how the river's mouth could have opened just enough to trap him beneath the ice. I thought how on his way to find what he expected to be his dead father, he could have been lost forever.

———

At the church suppers in Castine, Maine, three and a half hours from my home of origin, I often see my many aunts who are now deceased, stalwart women whose affection and goodwill lifted me up as a child. I have found a twin for every one of them. Aunt Anna, Aunt Bea, Aunt Verta, Aunt Rita, Aunt Marguerite, Aunt Ginny, Aunt Ethel, Aunt Nina, Aunt Elma. They still wear the starched, bibbed aprons of years ago, of sisterhood, of baking white cakes that rise up like castles and sweet rolls that are made for butter, of exchanging recipes, some for food and some for life. They are the women of good causes and of lives surely not quite what they dreamed they would be.

A few of these women are descendants of the Loyalists, just as I am. When some of my ancestors came north from Boston in the late 1700s, on their way to British territory, they landed on the shores of Castine. One story is that they thought they were on the St. Croix River in New Brunswick, Canada, and did not know they had landed on the Penobscot River, which was a day's sail south of their planned destination, and part of the United States. They built houses and planted crops, only to learn years later that they were not under the protection of the British Navy. Immediately, many of them dismantled their houses, loading them and their families and possessions on ships so they might sail north to the banks of the St. Croix River, then called the Quoddy.

One of the history books that I read as a child said the Loyalist men were gallant gentlemen who wore powdered wigs and plum-colored coats and three-cornered hats, and that on their ships, along with their slaves and livestock, they carried priceless mahogany, silver, damask linen, and family portraits in heavy trunks. When the Indians saw the white-sailed ships of the Loyalists on the horizon, they thought they were great birds coming across the water, for no ships had ever ventured that far along that river. So did the white man come to the waters of the Quoddy. There, they settled and named the town St. Andrews, Shiretown of Charlotte.

My family often visited St. Andrews. The Loyalist houses, which had been dismantled in Castine and rebuilt in St. Andrews, were marked with plaques, and my parents loved to walk by them and think of the Loyalists' journey from the Penobscot to the St. Croix.

"Imagine," Mom often said, "moving your whole life on a ship. What a job. Those poor women having to settle twice."

After Mom died, I found in the bottom of her hope chest two large linen pieces with red stitching. *Redwork*, it is called, and the pieces were stitched by my grandmother, Lenora Taylor, the one who died at Fairview, the one who was a descendant of those grand yet once-displaced Loyalists. Her Loyalist ancestors who remained in America were ancestors of the twelfth president of the United States, Zachary Taylor. Recently, *U.S. News and World Report* voted him one of the worst presidents ever to have served. Although he was a brave soldier, the article said, he could be "unaware to the point of innocence."

One of those pieces of redwork from the hope chest shows a young girl sleeping, accompanied by the stitched words WHEN I WAS YOUNG, I DREMED THAT LIFE WAS BEAUTY. I love that the word *dreamed* is spelled wrong. The second linen is of a young woman sweeping, with the words, BUT WHEN I WOKE, I FOUND THAT LIFE WAS DUTY.

One corner of the "duty" linen is frayed, probably discovered by a mouse, who no doubt wanted to line her new nest with red linen thread, working vigorously to retrieve it. I suppose most women end up working harder in their lives than they ever "dremed." I know many of my Loyalist ancestors did, as surely as my mother and my teacher-aunt, and those women of good causes and church suppers.

At my first church supper in Castine, a woman whom I likened to my Aunt Verta, because of her rotund, solid shape and smiling, tilted round face, welcomed me and later asked if I knew the story of the little drummer boy.

"The one who didn't have a present for Jesus?" I asked.

"Oh no," she said, "the one who was abandoned here in 1779. He was American, and when the British fled, they left him locked up in the barracks of Fort George." I pictured Fort George high on the hill. I had already explored it with Phoebe and Georgia, so I was familiar with the barred cell dug into the side of the hill.

"They say he played his drum until he died. When they excavated a number of years ago, they found a small skeleton drooped over a dusty drum."

"Really?" I said. The image took my breath away; not the image of a young boy dying, but the image of my ancestors, my blood, having abandoned him.

———

In the emergency room at the hospital in Blue Hill, Maine, where I have waited with each of my daughters as they spiked a temperature or cradled a broken arm, there is an extra-wide interior door that says ICU. Seeing it always reminds me of Stephen, who survived being shot in a field on a Halloween night, but who later lay behind such a door in a New Brunswick hospital. He was packed on a bed of ice and bleeding from every orifice of his body, dying at the age of twenty-two from prescribed drugs that had secretly ravaged his body, because of an undetected liver condition.

We, his family, had been instructed to say good-bye as he hemorrhaged, but Mom refused to say good-bye to one of her children, keeping a prayer vigil over him for twenty-four hours until his bleeding stopped and the doctor pronounced his obvious recovery a miracle. Dad stood behind Mom the whole time she quietly prayed, his hand resting on her shoulder like a flightless wing, but as far as I know, his legs never once buckled, the way they had when the doctor first announced Stephen's pending death.

Ten years after Stephen recovered, Dad would lie behind the same ICU door, his body refusing to heal after surgery for intestinal cancer. It would take days for the hospital staff to discover that a pair of surgical scissors had been left inside him, post-op. Recently I read the chances of this medical situation happening are one in fifteen thousand. A doctor who is a MacArthur recipient is studying such things in hopes of improving the odds against medical mistakes.

Reading it, I couldn't help but wonder what the odds were of having your car struck by a train, and what were the odds of surviving such a wreck? What were the odds of getting intestinal cancer at the age of fifty and then surviving the embedded surgical scissors for weeks? Such was our father's intestinal fortitude, we often teased, and he was so courageous and resolute that we never dreamed he'd really die. But thirty years after the surgical scissors were removed, he would once more lie behind that ICU door, his cancer having recurred so aggressively that it had eaten the bottom of his spine. Still, his fortitude remained, even though morphine kept him restless and sometimes confused.

"I can't remember your name," he said to me with glassy tears racing down his cheeks, the morning before he died. I was thirty-six years old, but felt as helpless as an infant.

We children had gathered with Mom for fifty-four days and nights, all of us taking turns keeping a vigil over Dad. We did not want him to die alone. The doctor had noticed a slight improvement, a rallying, and my family suggested that I take a break.

"You need to go home and sleep in your own bed," Mom said. "You're exhausted."

Before leaving, I asked the doctor how long he thought Dad would live.

"He's very sick," the doctor said, "but he's also very strong. His heart is like an athlete's."

No wonder. All those years of heading into un-trailed forests with a compass around his neck, several miles but a stroll for him.

Yet the night after I arrived back home in Maine, Evangeline called at 3:20 in the morning to say Dad was gone.

Dad. Tall and dark and limber.

"Jesus," I cried, "dear Jesus."

"He's all around you," Evangeline said. "Just feel him."

I did not know if she meant Jesus or Dad. I did not ask.

———

To this day I am often haunted by Dad's suffering and sorrows and how I contributed to some of them. One always occurs to me when I am on my way to Canada and pass the curving on-ramp along northbound 95 at Orono. It resembles the entrance ramp where two friends were killed on the night that we graduated from high school.

At the time of the accident, I was back at the party house, having refused to leave when my date coaxed me to go for an early breakfast at an all-night diner out on the Trans-Canada Highway. I don't know why I refused to go. My parents had warned me never to get in a car with a driver who had been drinking, but I was young and had already taken other chances. Had I accepted the offer, I too would have been hit by the oncoming tractor-trailer. My friend Carol sat between the two boys in that car and was killed instantly, along with her date, Greg.

The car crash was so loud that it woke residents along the river and a phone chain began, finally reaching Dad, who rushed to the site. The emergency crews had already removed the passengers, and the howl of the distancing ambulances could still be heard.

A friend at the site said that when my father saw the crumpled car, his knees buckled and he dropped down on the eroded treeless riverbank and wept. Of course, he recognized my date's car, and of course, he had no way of knowing I hadn't been in it.

———

When I was eighteen, I wanted nothing more than to escape my stretch of road with wrecked cars, barred windows, and ICU doors, first landing in Toronto, where I went to finishing school and then studied acting, and then, much later, after I was married, to Boston, and finally north, like my Loyalist ancestors, to Castine, Maine.

At eighteen, I wanted to leave the field of gunshots. I wanted to forget that my maternal grandmother had died in that mental hospital after she visited a Pentecostal church for the first time. During the service, a zealous young preacher had insisted she stand on a chair and try to speak in tongues. Why stand on a chair? None of us know, but perhaps like one of her infamous American ancestors, she too was unaware to the point of innocence, climbing on that unsteady chair as she was told. Soon, she fell, hitting the front of her head so hard on the altar that she began to convulse.

To clear himself, the preacher drove her to Fairview two hours away and told them, She's having a fit. She died a week later of a cerebral hemorrhage. She was forty-nine years old.

After my grandfather brought my deceased grandmother home, he laid her naked on their bed, studying every inch of the body that had given him nine children, the body that had been with him since she was a young woman, sleeping and *dreming* that life was beauty. She was the descendant of another woman who had once also unknowingly landed on the wrong shore.

Mom said that her father was afraid her mother had been beaten to death, as was often the custom in lockdown facilities. A police officer, he was aware of these things. He was also Scottish Catholic, and did not believe that people should attempt to speak in tongues. He died one month and one day later, while cutting firewood. According to Mom, he died of a broken heart, which was only a saying then, but recently has been proven to be a very real physical response to sudden loss. Maybe the doctor who proved that should get a MacArthur grant as well. For in this world of sorrow, proof of one's broken heart might be a worthy diagnosis, a condition to take precautions against.

At the time of my grandparents' deaths, their children ranged from two to twenty years of age, and were divided up like candy among their relatives and neighbors. Mom, who was the two-year-old, went to live with an aunt who was going blind. Uncle Rand became a painter like his mother, and later did many paintings of his siblings before they were split apart. My favorite is of all the siblings, bundled up for the winter cold and chopping wood outside. The boys hand-saw the wood while the little girls stack and secure it under their tiny chins as their colorful scarves blow sideways in the wind. In the frosty window of the small Cape behind them, a toddler's face peers out—Mom—and above her in another frosty pane is Aunt Anna, who eventually ended up at Fairview.

Watching her younger siblings, Aunt Anna must have felt their desire to stay together, their little hands and arms working so, to keep the fire going, still *dreming* of a life of beauty, yet already training for their lives of duty. Of course, she knew that keeping the family together would be impossible. She couldn't take care of them all. Mom said the unjustified feeling of abandoning her siblings never left Anna. And eventually she died of a broken heart, too, although some called it a heart attack instead.

———

Among the sorrows I wanted to forget was that when Aubrey finally reached Dad on the night of the train crash, he had vomited so badly that Dad had to strip his putrid outer clothes away. Afterward, Dad removed his own coat and gave it to Aubrey.

According to Aubrey, Dad said, It's only a few miles, let's keep walking. It will be good for us. And that is what I see when I remember that cold moonlit night: the back of a tall man in a fedora hat, his wing-shaped hand resting on the shoulder of a skinny-legged boy, in an oversized car coat. If I were a painter like my grandmother and uncle, I'm sure I would have already painted several variations of this scene. It is as real to me as if I'd been there, so real that sometimes I could reach out and touch it—not the scene so much, but the feeling I have imagining it.

Recently, I saw an Edvard Munch exhibit. I have always been drawn to his well-known painting, *The Scream*. Seeing it in a photograph for the first time many years ago, I had the same terrifying feeling as on that day when we sat in the visiting room with Aunt Anna at Fairview. In the background, Munch has used the orange of the waiting room, creating a speeding swirl of fear. The figures in *The Scream* are still, but the world around them is rippling out, as if a heavy stone had been thrown into a still pond.

Yet after the afternoon with Munch's work, I came to the conclusion that perhaps *The Scream* was one of his lesser works. Like the waiting room at the mental hospital, the painting had the feeling of horror without the balm of compassion. It was ghoulish in both its central image and the sound I imagined vibrating around it.

After, Munch's paintings *Death in the Sickroom* and *The Sick Child* were supreme in my estimation. In these paintings, love embraces the suffering. "I do not paint what I see, but what I saw," Munch said. "My sufferings are part of myself." And although the horror is present in these less-famous paintings, it is lessened by an echoing compassion, far more powerful than a sickening orange swirl. These paintings are neither spooky nor ghoulish.

As Munch's sister Sophie was dying, she asked to be taken out of a bed and put in a chair. Munch's *Death in the Sickroom* captures the emotion of that scene. "It's not the chair that should be painted," Munch wrote, "but what a person has felt at the sight of it."

In the painting, just the slight crook of Sophie's arm is visible. It is mainly the back of the high-styled chair she has been placed in that the viewer sees. To me, as in *The Scream*, it is a painting of echoes, but gentler, like a familiar hymn being hummed over and over. In a chair behind the dying girl sits another girl, red-headed as Sophie is, with her head bowed. Both of these figures are attended by somber yet obvious loving parental shapes. One shape is praying. There is the exquisite feeling of wholeness in this painting. Why, I wondered, standing before *Death in the Sickroom*, if one was going to admire a Munch painting, would one not admire this one? Why choose a scream rather than a hymn or a prayer?

———————

At eighteen, en route to Toronto, I wanted to forget that the man who shot my brother on Halloween night was our school bus driver. As a Halloween prank, a group of boys had wanted to let the air out of the school bus tires. What boys of twelve wouldn't want to do that? I'm sure in their giddy enthusiasm, it never crossed their minds that a gunman might lie in wait, nor that after shooting Stephen, this man would threaten to finish him off. "If you don't stop screaming, I'll take you to the river and drown you."

After a short trial, the shooter spent one night in jail, and then continued to drive my siblings and me and the other kids in our neighborhood to school. How I hated his pinpoint eyes, his round wire glasses, his beaky nose and black hole for a mouth, somehow even more threatening than a frozen river that could swallow a boy. How I avoided the sight of him when the bus door snapped open. How I wanted to run.

No wonder Stephen eventually left school, remaining home with Mom, who homeschooled him with such love and care that we siblings have often voted him the smartest of us all. She taught him to discuss his dreams and think in metaphor, she taught him to bake biscuits, to study religion and to recite poetry, and she taught him to love the sound of quiet and to read critically and to rest. And by listening to his anguish, she taught him to listen to the anguish of others, one of his traits that I now value most.

While in Toronto, I studied the Stanislavski acting method, which encourages one to visit their familiar emotions in order to give a character authenticity. As Maria in *West Side Story*, I reacted to the brother's death while recalling my own brother's bleeding body one Halloween night. I played Amanda Wingfield in *The Glass Menagerie*, thinking of my Aunt Anna and the sense of abandonment she must have felt on the day we drove away without her. Each time I used some deeply buried and difficult memory to elicit an emotion, I also grew closer to the character that I longed to create, and closer to my family's pain.

One day, an acting coach asked for joy rather than despair, and I found that emotion impossible to give.

"For God's sake," he said, "it's your middle name. Can't you give the character some joy?"

I felt paralyzed—held in a scream.

I thought of the word *joy*, saw its jumbled letters in front of me, and then scurried inside myself, looking for the precious thing tucked at the bottom. I remembered how my mother had given me the name Joy, because she had labored all night to give birth to me. When telling me of the morning I was born, she always quoted the chosen psalm, *Weeping may endure for a night, but joy cometh in the morning.*

Beneath my acting lay much joy, but my heart and mind refused to visit it. What if I wore my joy memories out, or rubbed them bare, as I had been doing with my difficult memories? I had allowed the echoes of my family's screams to repeat openly on stage, but my joy belonged to me.

That very day, I quit acting lessons and for a time took up modeling. On runways and photo shoots, I painted my face with such care that nothing of my past shone through. I learned to keep my eyes cool and concentrated. I learned to let clothing become the chameleon's skin, which allowed me to strut down a runway. Walking with loose hips, I felt all that truly mattered was still hidden deep inside. My joyful memories were like gardenias in a sealed room—unbelievably beautiful, and yet so pungent, they could make me weep whenever I opened the door.

Much later, and a week before Dad died, I spent the night at the hospital with him. He'd been moved from the ICU to Palliative Care. Disease had played hide-and-seek in Dad's body for many years, yet the odds had always worked in his favor, and so his medically predicted and pending death was impossible to accept. Hadn't he always survived? Hadn't we all?

The night light made his hospital room seem gray, yet somehow iridescent. Sitting beside him, it felt as if we were in the gloaming, as if time had been magically rolled back and the two of us were old friends sitting together on the branch of a big tree. We were suspended. *Held in love* is the only way to describe it.

In that hospital room, I leaned forward in the blue vinyl chair beside Dad's bed and rested my hands on the white sheets. He patted and rubbed my fingers as we talked, and I looked down at his still-tanned hands and his worn wedding band. It was as thin as golden wire. He and Mom had been married fifty-nine years. After a while, Dad moved over in his narrow hospital bed and made room for me. I knew it hurt him to move, but he didn't wince. I climbed in under the sheet and laid my head on his chest, listening. His heart was thumping like a distant drum, which I would come to remember as the slow steady beat of death, as ominous as the sound of a boy drumming in his deathly barrack.

Dad's emaciated hip bone curved into my stomach. He smelled of a pine forest.

"Your mother's eyes," Dad said. "I'm worried about her eyes."

Mom's macular degeneration no longer allowed her to drive her car or read her adored books. She sometimes missed a step and tripped.

"It just seems so unfair. I wish I could trade my good eyes for hers," Dad said.

"Daddy, we will take care of Mom."

He wrapped his arms around me tighter and held me close to his side, and I felt all of his lovely green forest coming from his wasted body into mine. I felt joy. I felt wholeness.

"And who will take care of you?" he asked.

I had long left modeling behind, and was married with a child of my own, living on the coast of Maine and writing. "My husband," I said.

"Yes," Dad said, "yes, Bill will."

He kissed my forehead, and I said, "Dad, will you sing 'A Bicycle Built for Two'?"

Not only had it been a song he often sang to my mother, but for my sixteenth birthday, he had bought me a bicycle built for two and we had ridden it late into the night, singing and laughing, as the summer cicadas' wings hummed in the air, a hymn that lit a string of golden lights between my heart and his.

Dad pulled me closer and started to sing, but then his voice cracked and he stopped, so I sang for him while his fingers drummed out the tune on my shoulder.

It won't be a stylish marriage,
I can't afford a carriage,
But you'll look sweet upon the seat
Of a bicycle built for two!

On the night that Aubrey and Dad walked home from the train crash, they entered the kitchen and stood for a moment like strangers. A rush of cold air came in with them. I was drawing a pile of decimated trees on white paper. The roots of the trees reached up to the heavens as if they were hands releasing a prayer. Mom was next to the kitchen window, starching and ironing pillowcases. She had been wondering about Dad's whereabouts for some time, glancing out the dark window as she ironed.

Looking at Dad and Aubrey, her lips slowly shaped in an o, and suddenly she rushed across the kitchen and wrapped her arms around them. Her white apron strings tied at her back were like ribbon around a gift. Aubrey began to cry, so I rushed into the circle and cried, too, and among us there was a feeling of great gratitude, even though things were yet to be explained. The fresh smell of Mom's starched apron was like a clean bed. And there was the feeling of joy. There was wholeness.

On the night that Stephen was shot, rather than wait for help to arrive, Dad carried him to the backseat of our family car and rushed him to the hospital. Mom remained home with Aubrey and me. The police had been called but had not arrived. Although no one said it, I think my parents felt that night that the world had turned on their family and become a dangerous place.

Aubrey and I lay with Mom in her bed, one on each side, crying and shaking while she brushed our foreheads and hummed a familiar hymn. I thought of the words as I listened: *It is well with my soul. It is well with my soul, it is well, it is well, it is well with my soul.*

The phone on the nightstand rang.

Aubrey and I turned rigid beside Mom as we listened to the bus driver's voice blaring through the receiver, threatening to come and kill us all.

"Mr. Bates," Mom said, sitting up straight in the bed, "if you have a little time on your hands now, I suggest rather than shoot any more children, you get down on your knees and pray for mercy."

She slammed the receiver and then cuddled back down and pulled us to her chest. She smelled of baking bread and her heart was racing, almost buzzing, like the wings of summer cicadas. Soon, she began to hum once again.

After a while I began to hum, and then Aubrey did, too, and for a time we were tucked beneath the wings of a loving, humming mother, suspended. The night rolled back to its gloaming, to the happy time before the world had turned on us.

Many years later, I would read about a troop of Boy Scouts on a camping trip in the Northwest Territories. I remember the location as being seventy miles from the capital of Yellowknife, although I'm not sure that is accurate. In the night, a grizzly bear entered their tent and began mauling one of the boys. The others in their terror began to hum and then the bear soon left the tent alone. I suppose their humming was no different than our mother's. Faced with the death of one child, she managed to keep her other children's fear at bay with humming, no different than a little drummer boy beating his drum, or a dying father tapping out a favorite tune on a daughter's shoulder.

In so many ways, Maine is New Brunswick's twin sister. They line up together, shoring each other like siblings. Like the settlers that landed in Castine in 1773, believing they were in Canada, I often think I am in Canada as well. The similar places I travel allow me to remember my past. In these settings, the jagged cracks of my family's lives are still visible, but more importantly, so is their joy. I see the iridescent gloaming in each familiar scene. It was not that Dad was almost killed by a speeding train, but that afterward, he walked with his hand on the shoulder of his shocked son. It is not that he lay dying a painful death in a hospital bed, but that he found the strength to move over and make room for a daughter so she could breathe in the fleeting green of him. It is not that my brother was shot, but that afterward, Mom hummed my frightened brother and me to sleep. It is not that my grandmother died an unnecessary death in an insane asylum, but that my grandfather retrieved and cared for her body. And it is not that Stephen lay dying, but that Mom prayed until there was hope, while Dad's reassuring hand rested on her shoulder. When my family and I look back, we do not see the dying brother, we hear the prayers like cicada wings in the air, and we feel the golden light of such devotion lit between our hearts.

Sometimes when we remember, we weep. Not because we are sad, but because we know joy. Our parents wove it in us like red linen thread in a nest. And what, dear Jesus, what were those wonderful odds?

As Munch said, it is not the death chair that should be painted, but what a person has felt at the sight of it. How sturdy those feelings make us. Like the roots of the great trees that held everything in place on the banks of the Saint John River, our parents' love supported our family's hardships, and it continues, for that kind of love never leaves; it is all around. We simply need to feel it.

ten

And if we can enter a place of wonder, can we also enter a place of warning,
be it through a dream or a vision?

*D*reaming and trapped in a tetanus fever, I walk through the dark toward
Eaton's Boatyard. The gravel road is wet and gritty, and the storm has blown a
late-night crowd into Dennett's. The patrons swarm the long bar, my commu-
nity cousins mingling with the sailors who have taken refuge for the night, their
eyes aglow. Smoke from frying seafood escapes through the kitchen's exhaust
and hangs in the mist below the outdoor light like a ghostly school of fish. The
smoke is tinged with the perfume of rugosa roses, relentlessly propagating nearby
in soil and sand, a small pile of rocks as good as a mulch pile to their sturdy and
determined roots. Like the locals, the roses hover at the edge of worn roads and
paths for the summer, but by fall, their rose-hip fruit will beckon, my daughters and I savoring each bite as if we have been deprived stowaways on a ship.

Beneath the restaurant's sign, I glimpse a woman standing in the long grass.
She is wearing a dark coat, wrapped in the fishy mist. I curve around a deep
puddle toward her, but even from a distance, I know that she is not familiar.
Castine harbors a number of these women, and on occasion one appears, only
to scatter quickly. Stories of them pass like trading cards among the locals.
Perhaps, the stories themselves momentarily create the image of these women
like manatees becoming mermaids.

Her dark hair hangs in shreds and her elongated face is as dry and craggy-
looking as tree bark. As I move toward her, there is the sudden and pungent
smell of urine as if she has been hiding for years, hibernating with her sorrows. She stares at me, but doesn't move. She appears trapped and entangled,
and she exudes a heaviness not of weight, but of shadows, layers and layers,
so dense that they create a feeling of wilderness.

Hello.

My greeting bounces off her like a June bug hitting an outdoor light, and then lands between us on the wet, rose-misted gravel, stung with rejection. I curve away, but she continues to watch me, her haunting eyes like eyes in a portrait. They seem to say, Go away.

Go away?

Does she think that I am a ghost, or is she a ghost, or could she be one of the diminutive peasant women that my mother mentioned, a Cannered Noz who scrubs linens as she prays for absolution for the dying? Was I dying? Is she here to warn me, or is she someone who has made a journey to reclaim something: a long-gone lover, a child, or something from one of the boxes in the attic at Eaton's Boatyard. Will her tongue finally touch the nectar of a loved one, the rescuing creosote that she dreamt of while hiding with her grief? Or might she be the image of what a woman becomes when she longs for her youth, or feels that her real life is taking place somewhere else? Could she be an etching from the wall of my very own consciousness, a premonition of what my restlessness could bring? Or might I be making the transition from a year-rounder to a local? Are the ghosts beginning to reveal themselves to me, because I am now familiar to them? *Here I have been, among their shadows.*

A wind erupts and the bell buoy at the harbor's entrance begins its cavernous chime, the sound as lonely as a loved one's grave. Turning, I see that she is gone—a ghost of chance, a ghost of possibility—the long grass where she stood now swaying like mermaid's hair. Did I see her? Or did I create her by scratching at my own past? Or might she be the ghost of a lovesick woman? What is it that love dares the self to do? *Love dares the self to leave itself behind, to enter into poverty.*

Near Max's little beach is the spicy scent of lupine spray, extracted by the pounding rains, and now waltzing with the rose mist. Like the roses, the lupines are proliferating on the embankments and at the edges of village yards and through the fields across the causeway, their spirally pink and purple and white flowers standing like bridesmaids at a wedding. To breathe in their earthy scent is to believe that nothing bad could ever happen. It is the dug earth of both beginnings and endings, and it placates fear the way hope soothes away a pending loss.

Seawater has covered the beach and risen up to creep like a black cloak over the pilings that keep the road from collapsing. When the night sea recedes, wrack and flotsam will mark its high tide. Eventually the torn rockweed will be decimated by the June heat, its olive-shaped air bladders and glistening branches drying to a crisp.

The pay phone at the boatyard rings, a loud shrill muffled by the winds like a woman's scream covered by a hand. I don't know if the ringing is a beckoning or a warning, but I know that I want to answer it, be it a mother, a lover, or a child. I remember my mother's siren-like voice, and wonder what prayers of intercession she would pray for me now. What instructing tales would she resurrect? I imagine picking up the phone and hearing my own voice coming back to me, lost and floating in orbit since the day she died. *Wait, not yet, Mom, I'm not ready.*

There is only dial tone, steady and crackling. Still, I want to say hello, but it is not forthcoming. It lies behind me on the wet gravel, having been wasted on a vision. The deserted-word feeling is far worse than the frustration I had when unable to speak clearly as a child. It is as if something that I love is wrapped in a word that has now departed, girl. Sparing me a line from Thoreau sprouts like a coaxed seedling, *Here I have been these forty years of learning the language of these fields that I may better express myself.*

Hello, hello . . .

. . . but nothing.

Nothing.

Hanging up the telephone, I keep both hands on its black and fetal curve, praying for it to ring again. Just one more time. *Please, let me speak to my mother.*

The night is still and humid, and the smell of roses and lupines is being sucked away and overcome with all that rots at the edge of the sea, soaked tarry cedar pilings and decaying barnacles and urchins and sculpins tangled in the lacy bryozoans. It is the bloating smell of a thousand drownings, the letting go of life.

You can smell it.

Words that have been knotted in my throat release. Mom is dead. She's dead. A heavy sweat breaks and percolates up through the soil of me like a poison. Tears come in one gulp. They are forceful and determined and knowing. They are not for the mother that I knew, but for the one who has moved beyond to become myth. The mother of wonder, the doe that now runs with velvet antlers.

A dog barks nearby and I cling to the phone, picturing the feral mongrel that my father came across while cruising, the dog that Mom likened to a mythic church grim: a black dog wandering through stormy nights, protecting the dead from the Devil. But who were the dead? And why was it that most myths told of protecting the dead rather than the living?

"You using the phone?" a man asks.

Turning, I am relieved to see the two sailors that swatted at Jinx earlier. My relief momentarily forgives them. The thinner one, Puck, is standing very close to me, and the fatter one is standing back, as if assessing the situation, his thumbs hooked in his jeans.

"No, go ahead," I say, backing away.

"Oh, we don't want to use it. We were just wondering if you're okay. You sound upset. What's wrong?"

The question is personal and registers as such. The smell of diesel lives on Puck like crude on a distressed falcon, and he has the slack-jaw speech of a Bahamian. I wonder if they might be drug-runners, if that battered wooden yawl that they sailed in on earlier is lined with things that are measured in grams and pounds and kilos, the very kind of boat that my husband would tell me to stay away from. *Don't go looking for trouble.*

"I was just passing and heard the phone ringing," I say.

The larger sailor grins like a pack dog. Might he be the dog that I just heard? Might the sharp bark of his soul precede him like a warning? And has my lost intuition finally returned? To waken me.

"Does it ring a lot?" Puck asks.

"Yes."

He nods slowly. "You from 'round here?"

"Yes, I am."

And in saying it, I feel some safety. Who would dare touch a local? But locals were touched all the time, just as my once-local schoolmate had been in that joint's bathroom. Her blue eyes vacant yet brimming return to me, and I know that what I was unable to define so long ago were pools of viciousness. They cradled the savageness that had been bestowed upon her. *All aggression, whether it comes from man or from the world, is of animal nature.*

I want to run, but which way? Past the two men, back toward Dennett's and the locals, or behind and up the stairs with the broken step toward my family? I know that these men could make my eyes brim, or worse, they could turn me into a ghost wandering about the village, looking for my loved ones. These were expert *venatores*; surely, a gaggle of decapitated ostriches lay in their wake.

"How 'bout a drink?" Puck sways as if his spine has been replaced with the long-stalked kelp that sways beneath deep water, its tensile strength able to withstand both pulling and pounding. "We got gin on the boat. C'mon. Come with us."

"I've got to get home. My family is waiting."

Puck tilts his head as if *family* is a word that he doesn't recognize. His stare is blurry-looking, suggesting the hazy way he sees me. A woman is a woman is a woman.

"C'mon, pretty lady," he burps. "We'll bring you back."

The sudden tension in the air not only harvests the stench of sea rot, but of wet granite, which smells of brimstone. Fear rises, and I taste its bitter yeast, knowing the bread of me will be nothing in the jaws of these men. Later their slack-jaw talk will spew me from their memory like dust from a wafer. Another night will take them to another place, another story, another spewing of crumbs.

If I could be a bird, I would be a cormorant. If I were a cormorant, I would have known to lift off earlier. Ancient truth would have told me, but my instincts have been dulled by my own musings, my wings soiled with the black crude of ego, trapping me in the purgatory of duality, the musing of running or staying.

Go away . . .

I run toward the stairs, trying to concentrate on my one advantage. That third missing step. The one that Kenny hasn't had time to fix. I will know to step over it, but they will not.

"Hey," someone hollers, "*stop.*"

"HEY."

When I reach the top step, I turn. A flashlight is moving from the door of Eaton's Boatyard. It hitches up and down with Kenny's walk. He circles the beam on the two men like a lasso.

"What's going on here, boys?" He stops in front of the men who are now at the bottom of the steps, and he switches the light back and forth on their faces.

"Nothin'. We were just asking this lady if she wanted to have a drink." There is a leering smile in Puck's answer, a subtle feeler to see if Kenny wants to run with the pack. The words crawl over my skin. Kenny flashes the beam up the stairs and it lies on my feet like sheer gossamer, like the never-spoken rule of launchings: *Do not touch her unnecessarily.*

"Get down here," he demands. I know that he is faking brotherhood for the sake of tension and his own enjoyment. I imagine the tango building and I think, Here we go. Kenny is going to rumble with these creeps, and I'm going to be right in the middle of it.

"C'mon," he hollers.

———

Standing beside him, he shines the flashlight into Puck's squinting eyes. The sailor's grinning lips are parched. One front tooth is chipped, and near the gum, it has turned as dark as tar. His eyes are pinpoint blue and red-rimmed with what appears to be more gin than tonic. When Kenny first put the light on him, Puck pushed his hands down into his pockets like spikes and his posture turned stiff, but now he has gained some brotherly anticipation, and his posture has loosened.

Kenny shines the light in the other sailor's face. His eyes look cool and glisten like an animal in an alleyway. "Tell me, boys, what did the lady tell you when you invited her for a drink? What did she say?"

They glare mean drunkenness. For a moment, all smells and sounds are gone, just as they were on the day that my brother and I were almost run over by that speeding car. Everything left as if a tunnel from heaven was beaming down on us, wanting to take us.

"Get the hell out of here," Kenny says. He steps back, and then uses the flashlight like a policeman directing traffic around an accident scene.

The sailors don't move.

I consider running up the stairs again, but again I am held in that purgatory of duality, in the decision of running or staying. Why? Clearly, these men could still set a match to their wayward desires and win. And clearly my survival story would not be one that I had chosen to claim and then recount like a charming tale, but rather one that had chosen to claim me, my eyes forever brimming with their savageness. Why had I walked through the dark boatyard? Why had I taken an unnecessary chance? Why?

Kenny shines the light on Puck's face and says, "G'wan, git."

Puck gathers phlegm in his throat and spits on my face. He smirks, *Whore*, and then turns, walking away, his sidekick following him and mumbling.

Kenny keeps the light on their staggering backs. When they disappear beyond the dock, and the motor of their dinghy revs up and then fades toward their boat, Kenny says, "Why were you talking to those bottom-feeders?"

"I wasn't talking to them," I say, wiping my face of the spit.

"Yes, you were. I heard'cha."

"I was just answering their questions."

"You don't answer questions. This isn't goddamn Shangri-la," Kenny says. "A couple of assholes like that could ruin a girl's life."

Girl?

He walks away as gruff as a goat, flicking his flashlight off. There's no need for him to see his way. The map of him memorized his little road long ago. He has spurned all wealth beside.

The sky had taken on a dark and crimson sheen, the color that blood is when it mixes with dirt. It matches the gritty shame that I feel. Why?

Because I sinned, I hear my mother say on that day in the nursing home, her opened palm resting on her lap as if there lay all the narratives of those she loved.

But I saw nothing.

Nothing.

What was it she wanted me to see?

Each step I take after the broken step brings another regret, an embarrassing list that I could only share with someone capable of forgiving me.

When I cross Water Street and start up Green Street, I think I hear a girl crying, but the sound is so faint and distant that I cannot be sure. She sobs as if she is mourning. The Cannered Noz? My mother? My aunts? Or is it the single echo of every girl and every woman? Of all the guilt that gathers over the years, every hello and good-bye—*Ciao.*

Kenny's truck rumbles up beside me. His face is lit red by the dashboard's lights. "You all right?"

I want to say no. I want to tell him that I hear crying and that it is scaring me. I want to tell him that I have been a stranger to myself and therefore estranged from others, but I know that he would balk at that. I want to tell him that I've fallen in love with a cormorant, but that cormorant won't give me the time of day. I want to confess that by sometimes feeling my life is somewhere else, waiting to begin, I have been ignoring the life that I have. The life taking place. I have sometimes floated outside it, estranged, and unable to break through to the here and now. I have lived in a dream.

And what was the here and now made of? The sweet and golden honey of all that had been lovingly bestowed. This was the balm for the torn and hidden hole that held my losses. That was what Mom had wanted me to see in her open palm. Nothing. Losses were nothing. It was what one procured from the hole they left that mattered. It whispered through the pines and through the sea and on the wind, and when all else failed, it stood before one with outstretched wings. *Know me.*

I ask Kenny if he can tell me anything about *Anne of Castine.*

"The boat?"

"Yes."

"My father built her. I still got the patt'n for her at the boatyard."

Patt'n, I think. Why would his father have taken out a patent on a boat? It doesn't fit the Eaton mold. And then it becomes clear. Pattern. The word is *pattern.* My oversight is jolting. Are these not my adopted people? Do I not pride myself on understanding their inflections and intentions?

Here I have been these forty years . . .

"Some of her wood is the same wood they used to make Cuban cigar boxes. She's had some rough times, but she's still a beauty."

I say, "Who?"

"Anne, for Lord sake—who else have we been talking about?"

"Who owns her?" I ask.

"A pilot from Orono. Hell of a nice guy."

A pilot. A pilot.

"You're not crying 'bout a boat, are ya?"

"It's not about a boat," I say.

"What is it, then?"

"I've made some mistakes, that's all."

"Mistakes. Forget about them. Do you want a drive up the hill or not?"

"I'm good," I say.

Kenny nods, waving his hand once as if chopping the air, and then speeds off.

Walking on, I whisper the word good again, knowing that was my original wish for myself. To be a good girl. Good. It occurs to me that the word, like love, flows from a greater source, and it is a choice. Something that you do again and again, whether you feel like it or not.

———————

Our porch light is on, swinging gently like a man holding a lantern. Walking up the wet and shiny brick walk, I tell myself that everything in my past needs to be remembered. Lined up with my family's bestowed stories. No matter what. They are my life's passport, stamped and stained with my ancestors' loves and losses, and they are an antidote to this world.

Beside the front door is a pile of our daughters' painted rocks. Some with birds, some with beach scenes, some with towering green trees, and some with red crosses drawn on deep blue backgrounds. They have left them here to be played with tomorrow. Their sleeping faces beckon me, their gardenia musk a breath of necessary absolution. They hold my story, my two selves. They are my sweet settling twice.

See, you have been carved in the palm of my hand.